DANISH YEARBOOK
OF
PHILOSOPHY

VOLUME 45

DANISH YEARBOOK OF PHILOSOPHY

VOLUME 45
2010

MUSEUM TUSCULANUM PRESS
UNIVERSITY OF COPENHAGEN 2012

Published for
Dansk Filosofisk Selskab
in cooperation with
the Philosophical Societies of Aarhus and Odense
and with financial support from
the Danish Research Council for the Humanities

*

EDITORIAL BOARD:

FINN COLLIN
University of Copenhagen

JØRGEN HUGGLER
Danish University of Education

UFFE JUUL JENSEN
University of Aarhus

STIG ANDUR PEDERSEN
Roskilde University

HANS SIGGAARD JENSEN
Copenhagen Business School

MOGENS PAHUUS
Aalborg University

LARS GUNDERSEN
University of Aarhus

*

Articles for consideration and all editorial communications should be sent in three copies to:
Danish Yearbook of Philosophy
University of Copenhagen, Department of Philosophy
Njalsgade 80, DK 2300 Copenhagen S, Denmark

Business communications, including subscriptions and orders for reprints, should
be addressed to the publishers:
MUSEUM TUSCULANUM PRESS
Njalsgade 126
DK 2300 Copenhagen S
Denmark

*

© 2012 DANISH YEARBOOK OF PHILOSOPHY
COPENHAGEN, DENMARK
PRINTED IN DENMARK
BY SPECIALTRYKKERIET Viborg A-S

ISBN 978 87 635 3753 7
ISSN 0070 2749

CONTENTS

Søren Flinch Midtgaard: *Moral Arbitrariness and Global Justice* .. 7–28

Kaj Børge Hansen: *Conceptual Foundations of Operational Set Theory* 29–50

Christian Beenfeldt: *Knowing Oneself? An Essay on Comtean Skepticism about Introspective Self-Observation* 51–70

Lars Östman: *Agamben. Naked Life and Nudity* 71–88

Nikolaj Nottelmann: *A Critique of Laurence BonJour's Central Arguments for a priori Fallibilism* 89–105

MORAL ARBITRARINESS AND GLOBAL JUSTICE

SØREN FLINCH MIDTGAARD

Aarhus University

Abstract

Cosmopolitans claim that nationality is plausibly a factor that is arbitrary from a moral point of view on a par with, for example, talents, sex, and color. Accordingly, they believe that principles of justice designed to neutralize or mitigate arbitrary inequalities have global scope. Critics, otherwise friendly to the moral presumption against arbitrary differences, point out that this presumption only achieves moral relevance within the context of domestic institutions. They emphasize especially the legally coercive nature of the latter. The paper examines the following avenues for accounting for the asserted profound moral significance of domestic coercive structures (as opposed to international structures, coercive or otherwise): (i) domestic structures impose coercion in the name of its subjects, and they are asked to accept this coercion on moral grounds; (ii) domestic coercion is profound; (iii) domestic coercion is direct or immediate; (iv) domestic coercion is paradoxical in the sense that it infringes, but at the same time is a precondition for individual autonomy; (v) and/or domestic coercion is autonomy-infringing. I find each of these grounds seriously wanting. In particular, some properties which domestic institutions plausibly have and which plausibly trigger the presumption against arbitrary inequalities are shared by international or global institutions; and other properties which differentiate the two institutional structures are not morally significant in such a way that the objection to arbitrary inequalities is only relevant with respect to domestic institutions.

Introduction

The argument for substantial egalitarian or prioritarian conclusions appealing to the claim that inequalities in distributive shares caused by natural and social contingencies are arbitrary from a moral point of view plays a key role in John Rawls' *A Theory of Justice*.[1] While Rawls himself for various reasons restricted the application of the argument from arbitrariness to the domestic domain, early responses to *A Theory of Justice* extended the argument to the international or global level, observing that nationality is plausibly a factor that is arbitrary from a moral point of view on a par with, for example, talent, sex, and color.[2] In the recent literature on global justice the argument from moral arbitrariness continues to be important, especially among cosmopolitans.[3] Consider Simon Caney's recent forceful statement:

> Which state someone belongs to is, in many cases, a matter of luck. It is a matter of fortune whether someone is born into Berkshire or Bihar and it seems highly perverse to argue that such facts should affect what people are entitled to. Why, one may ask, should being born into one state have such a tremendous impact on people's prospects in life? It is hard to see why something so arbitrary—as arbitrary as one's class origin or social status or ethnic identity—should be allowed to have such normative implications.[4]

Whilst the argument from arbitrariness unites important strands of cosmopolitan thinking in contemporary international ethics, a particular resistance of this argument, or the appropriate scope of this argument, is the common ground of a series of profound recent contributions. The thrust of the latter is the belief that the argument from arbitrariness is basically sound, but that its soundness depends upon a certain institutional or societal relation obtaining. The relevant institution is believed to be the state, especially its *legally coercive*[5] structure. Legally coercive structures, the argument goes, must be justified to those subjected to them. Such structures can only be justified in so far as their construction does not allow arbitrary inequalities, or at least only allows such inequalities if they benefit the worst off.[6] The main representatives of this view are Michael Blake and Thomas Nagel.[7]

The present paper sets out to rebut Blake's and Nagel's arguments for the restricted application of the presumption against inequalities that are arbitrary from a moral point of view. It does so by arguing that some properties which national institutions have and which plausibly give rise to principles of justice that neutralize or mitigate arbitrary inequalities, global institutions also have thus making similar principles appropriate; other properties in virtue of which domestic and international structures may be said to differ are not morally significant in such a way that principles of justice are only relevant within domestic institutions.

The paper proceeds by examining in turn the arguments of the two main representatives for the view under consideration. Hence I scrutinize Nagel's and Blake's arguments in turn. The latter assessment is structured in accordance with different suggestions as to how the asserted moral significance of coercive structures could be accounted for.

Thomas Nagel

Nagel's account focuses on the special justificatory situation which arguably arises, and only arises, within the coercive institutions of a sovereign state. He emphasizes that people, without being given a choice, are subject to these coercive structures.[8] Furthermore, the coercion is imposed in their name. People are in a sense authors of the coercive power.[9] Finally, the citizens to whom coercive constraints apply are expected to accept these constraints on moral grounds—to regard them as justified. The conception of political power or of a political association suggested seems clearly Rousseauian, depicting individuals both in the role as law givers (or Citizens) and as ruled by these constraints (being Subjects) and as achieving freedom or autonomy in virtue of their acceptance of the coercive constraints.[10] Now a special justificatory situation arises within an association of this kind, according to Nagel, because individuals, if they are to take responsibility for these constraints as their joint authors and to endorse them on moral grounds, must be provided with a justification including a justification of eventual accompanying inequalities that are arbitrary from a moral point of view. Such a justification with universal application including to those most disadvantages by arbitrary inequalities, the argument proceeds, is not forthcoming unless coercive structures and the way in which they organize the complex of social and economic institutions take significant measures to redress undeserved inequalities. If they are justified at all, then it is only on the grounds that the worst off would be even worse off if the inequalities in question were not allowed.[11]

The institutions of a given state also coerce outsiders, for example, in virtue of its immigration policies. Such coercion, however, does not, according to Nagel, give rise to a special justificatory situation of the kind arising with regard to domestic institutions. Whilst outsiders are, without having a choice, subject to the coercive institutions of a given community (poor citizens of another country face, for example, without having a choice, coercive measures of a state that would want to prevent them from accessing its labor market), and these institutions permit inequalities that admittedly are arbitrary from a moral point of view, the coercion is not undertaken in their name, and they are not expected to accept it on moral grounds. Hence, Nagel suggests, no justification is required, at least not of a kind that involves appeal to egalitarian or prioritarian principles of distributive justice.[12]

As we have seen, Nagel's argument is based on an alleged disanalogy between the domestic sphere and the international or global sphere;[13] in the former sphere as opposed to the latter, coercive institutions calling for justification obtain, and they can only be justified if they are constructed in such a way that they work to the maximal benefit of the worst off. Pace Nagel I aim to show that institutions calling for justification (a justification that is only forthcoming if the institutions are appropriately equalizing) obtain at the international or global level as well. To argue this point I draw on a real-life case mentioned in David Miller's recent book, namely the fences erected by the Spanish authorities to keep out African immigrants trying to get into Europe through Melilla, a tiny Spanish enclave on the North African coast that borders on Morocco.[14] Here we have an almost perfect case of pure prevention[15]—that is, barriers which make it almost impossible to break the immigration laws of the Spanish state. Only at severe risk to themselves may immigrants attempt to pass this barrier and if they succeed they almost certainly face harsh treatment by the Spanish authorities and finally deportation to their home countries. These immigration policies apply to outsiders who have no choice and the policies permit inequalities that are arbitrary from a moral point of view (the deprived African immigrant is much worse off than a Spanish citizen through no fault or choice of his own); inequalities which are especially to the detriment of poor outsiders.[16] Thus it seems proper for these immigrants to ask the specific country denying them access to justify its stance,[17] or for countries collectively to justify the global institutional structure pertaining to immigration that they help sustain. And if we grant Nagel's egalitarian intuition with respect to the requirements to such a justification, it will not be forthcoming unless the institutions are rearranged to neutralize or mitigate substantially arbitrary differences between the individuals to whom they apply. Institutionally, this may mean fairly open borders and/ or non-stingy redistributive measures according to appropriate egalitarian principles. If, in reply to this request on the part of the immigrants, we say, as Nagel proposes we should, that the coercion in question is not imposed in the name of the immigrants and that we do not ask them to accept it, then it seems that we would in effect be adding insult to injury. Think of a domestic analogy in which a government imposes coercion on all within its territory, but claims not to do so in the name of a certain minority severely disadvantaged by the coercion exercised. It seems clear that we would regard this as a blatant case of unjust treatment partly in virtue of it not showing equal respect and concern for the disadvantaged minority, not as something that somehow implies that the government needs not justify its acts by appeal to and in consistency with principles of egalitarian or prioritarian justice.[18] It is not clear then that the factor Nagel points to pertaining to the attitude of the coercing institutions carriers the moral weight he claims it does. Especially, it is not clear that it somehow overrides or implies the irrelevance of the intuition that arbitrary inequalities are morally problematic and should be neutralized or mitigated. The moral factor that stands out in the case of immigration policies hence seems to be the pervasive and unequalizing effects of the institutional structures which in a very real sense apply to the immigrants. Justice plausibly applies to acts and institutions with pervasive and profound non-culpable effects on the distribution of benefits and burdens. It is hard to believe that it is silent with respect to immigration policies. Note that Nagel would not, apparently, deny the unequalizing material consequences of coercively imposed immigration policies. He denies, however, that they, as opposed to the coercion exercised by domestic institutions, call for justification. This is not the case in that coercively enforced immigration policies, as opposed to domestic coercion, are not being imposed in the name of the subjects of coercion. According to my argument, what lends plausibility to the idea that imposition of coercive structures makes a justification appropriate are the unequalizing material effects of such structures, not whether those affected by the structures are asked to accept the structures. A sincere version of the latter request, and a willingness to construct institutions so that they are truly acceptable to all affected, is appropriate given the material effects of the coercive structures; it is not the case that the former is a condition for the latter to be in need of a justification.[19] The upshot of my argument against Nagel is then that the cases of domestic and international coercion should be treated similarly meaning that the structures in each case should work to the maximal benefit of the worst off representative if they are to be justified. Whether this, in the global case, suggests a case for open borders depends on the complex question whether such a policy is part of the global institutional scheme which better than alternative feasible schemes promotes the interests of the worst off.

Michael Blake
Blake's argument

Michael Blake defends another coercion-based account for the limited writ of the moral presumption against inequalities that are arbitrary form a moral point of view.[20] His argument revolves around a Razian notion of autonomy,[21] according to which "autonomous agents are understood to be part authors of their own lives; the autonomous person is able to develop and pursue self-chosen goals and relationships."[22] Among the preconditions for such autonomous agency thus understood to obtain, Blake emphasizes especially the absence of coercion or the incompatibility of coercion with autonomous agency. Given that an autonomous life is one that is directed by the agent's own will, coercion is an affront to this idea. First, coercion subjects the will of an agent to that of another. It does so by making a specific option, the one the coercer prefers, seem most attractive to the person being coerced by making alternative actions difficult or impossible to pursue.[23] Second, by doing so, coercion reflects "an attitude of disrespect, of infantilization of a sort inconsistent with respect for human agents as autonomous, self-creating creatures."[24] Whilst restriction of options is not as such, as long as a certain threshold of adequate options is in place, morally problematic, according to this view, restriction of options due to coercion is for the stated reasons: "there is a world of difference between becoming a doctor because it seems the best option realistically open to me, and becoming a doctor because someone else has made it the best option open to me by making other choices difficult or impossible to pursue."[25] Only in the latter case would I, and my will, to the detriment of my autonomy, be subjected to the will of another.

State structures, Blake submits, are essentially coercive in the autonomy-infringing way indicated above. Criminal and civil laws involve the imposition of the will of judges, acting on behalf of society, on other human beings.[26] For example, they make alternatives to paying taxes prohibitively difficult or costly. Thus they are prima facie morally problematic in the light of the important value of autonomy. Stated differently, they face a crucial justificatory burden. It must be shown that the coercive structures involved are acceptable to each and every one of those to whom they apply, including those most disadvantaged by the arbitrary differences which coercive social institutions may permit. Analogous to Nagel's Rawlsian view, to be universally justified, including to the least advantaged, the complex of coercive structures should be justified by reference to an impartial procedure the plausible upshot of which is principles which only permit arbitrary inequalities to the extent that they benefit the worst off maximally. Furthermore, this crucial justificatory burden giving rise to egalitarian or prioritarian principles is only relevant with respect to the institutions of the state and in relation to its own citizens. Internationally, coercion goes on as well, as Blake admits, but it is not of a type that infringes autonomy, or it does not do so in a way that gives rise to justification by appeal to egalitarian or prioritarian principles. Only a sufficitarian principle obtains at that level, according to Blake. Blake is very brief on this crucial claim regarding a disanalogy between domestic and international coercion. He indicates, however, different avenues for a defense of the distinction. I critically survey these avenues and suggest one myself, which I believe is initially more promising, but end up rejecting the various suggestions. None of them seem to provide a satisfactory ground for claiming that egalitarian or prioritarian principles of justice are appropriately restricted to the domestic sphere.

The profoundness of domestic coercion

Blake's first suggestion is that domestic coercion is particularly profound and thus autonomy-infringing. This is implied by his elaborated account for the legally coercive structure of the state, especially civil and penal law, and its powers over citizens—a structure which does not obtain globally. It is also suggested in a chapter of his on immigration:

> The state can do powerful things to all and only those who live within the sphere of authority: citizens may be taxed, punished, coerced, and in the limit case even executed by their own government. Unless foreign citizens perform some special act to put themselves within the government's sphere of influence, they are immune from such coercive actions.[27]

I find the claim that foreigners are only profoundly affected by the immigration policies of rich nations if they "perform some special act to put themselves within the government's sphere" (as in the case of the African immigrants trying to enter Spanish territory) unconvincing.[28] The fact that rich nations guard their borders to the extent of exercising a form of pure prevention implies that they are instrumental in not allowing large numbers of individuals to escape severely disadvantageous circumstances. This is at least in part a result of the coercion pertaining to immigration policies, and the inequalities they give rise to are in the standard case non-culpable. It seems to me that this conclusion would still be valid under circumstances of a global sufficitarian threshold. Even if satisfied this would still allow profound inequalities that are arbitrary from a moral point of view and this state of affairs would be closely linked to the immigration policies obtaining. Thus I believe that the claim for a disanalogy between domestic and international levels in terms of profound effects of coercion is a non-starter.[29] It might, however, matter morally whether for example the individual rich country intends that foreigners should have no option apart from residing in a country with meager wealth-producing facilities and in this way subjects them to its will to the detriment of autonomy. I address this suggestion below.

The direct or immediate nature of domestic coercion

The second suggestion alluded to by Blake is that domestic coercion is distinctive in virtue of its direct or immediate nature.[30] In his most explicit statement: "[O]nly the former [domestic legal institutions] engage in *direct* coercion against individuals, of the sort discussed above in connection with the criminal and civil law".[31]

As it stands, this ground for the distinction between domestic and international coercion seems doubtful. First, it is unclear that internationally no immediate or direct coercion of the kind Blake has in mind is taking place. Blake apparently associates direct coercion with clear instances of one person's plans and pursuits being replaced by those of another.[32] Such coercion is, according to Blake, most clearly found in the institution of criminal punishment, for example in terms of incarceration or even capital punishment, but also in civil law, for example in contract law, property law, and taxation.[33] But it seems that, for example, the African immigrants in the Melilla case mentioned above encounter precisely an instance of coercion in which their will are being subjected to that of another. Indeed, the ordinary law-abiding Spanish citizen is unlikely ever to be confronted with state powers that interfere in the same way with their autonomous pursuits. Of course we may say that the immigrant brings these consequences upon himself by trying to enter a foreign territory. Given deep inequalities of a non-culpable nature obtaining internationally, and that this state of affairs is not ruled out even if a sufficitarian threshold obtains, this seems rather lame to say; it is not clear that the option of staying home may be considered adequate.

This leaves open, of course, the possibility that domestic coercion is in some sense more direct than international coercion and that this makes justification in virtue of egalitarian or prioritarian principles appropriate in the former but not in the latter case. I question below, however, through considering various versions of the distinction between direct and indirect coercion, the claim that justification by appeal to egalitarian or prioritarian principles are appropriate in the former but not in the latter case.

Consider first the distinction between, on the one hand, subjecting someone to one's will by for example punishing him, or threatening to punish him, if he fails to comply; and, on the other, overriding his autonomous agency by inculcating in him norms which make him act the way you want.[34] It is unclear, I believe, on which ground we could say that the former makes appropriate a demand for impartial justification by appeal to egalitarian or prioritarian principles while the latter does not. In each case the agency of one person is substituted by the agency of another thus infringing autonomy, and there is no apparent reason one might wish to distinguish between the two cases in terms of degree of infringement. In Tolstoy's Anna Karenina, for example, the autonomy of the main character is slowly undermined by a process the linchpin of which is arguably the sexist moral standards of society: standards which suggest that it is especially wrong for a wife to leave her husband for another partner and require women to assume primary responsibility for the care of children and to do so within the confines of marriage. These standards take control of Anna Karenina's life after she has left her husband in that she cannot resist their socializing pressure especially as the challenges to her new life accumulate; they question her way of life, and she begins to question it herself. In brief, her self-respect is undermined to the extent that her chosen pursuits appear worthless. In consequence, she chooses to end all her autonomous pursuits, that is, commit suicide. No, or not much, direct coercion is going on, but this does not seem to make the process less painful and humiliating (than it would have been had elements of direct coercions been in play). Hence it is unclear why such indirect infringements of autonomy do not require a justification that is impartially and universally acceptable to those subjected to it. That is, it is unclear why indirect coercion, as opposed to direct coercion, does not make egalitarian or prioritarian principles of justice relevant.

A second distinction runs between, on the one hand, the restriction of an individual's options by a coercer the identity of which is known by the person being coerced and where the precise nature of the coercion exercised is open to view (meaning that the effect of the coercer on the option set of the person being coerced is vivid), and, on the other, the case in which the coercer acts at a distance from the person he coerces in the sense that the latter is not aware of the identity of the coercer or of being coerced at all and hence may not be aware of the precise nature of the coercion. The former kind of coercion may be considered direct and the latter indirect. Again, I fail to see that the two types of coercion are morally distinct in the sense that the former, but not the latter, calls for impartial and universal justification, that is, a type of justification which plausibly invokes considerations of equality or priority. In both cases the autonomous agency of the person being coerced is effectively undermined whether or not the coercion is in this sense direct or indirect and this appears to call for an impartial justification. In Dickens' Great Expectations the options of the main character are significantly affected by another person in an indirect way as indicated above. Remarkably, the options faced by the former (apart from the option of living one's life from within including being reflectively aware of the influences one discards or acts on) are in fact improved; but still, a life lived in this way, that is, in the dark concerning a crucial influence on one's choices, seems to be tainted in a disturbing way raising the utmost concern of autonomy.

Third, we may distinguish between the restriction of the option set of an individual performed by another in a face-to-face setting, and the restriction of the option set of an individual by others through impersonal channels such as the market.[35] This is a theme in Marx' work forming part of his ground for distinguishing between feudal and capitalist exploitation. Marx' treatment of the two kinds of exploitation plausibly suggests that exploitation of the impersonal kind is at last as morally problematic as exploitation of the personal kind is. While the former is indeed exploitative, it is openly so. Specifically the ratio of necessary to unnecessary labor is public. Necessary labor is given by the number of days the serf works for himself and his family, unnecessary labor by the number of days he works for his master. In capitalist exploitation, by contrast, this ratio is obscure to the degree that workers and others may be misled to think that unnecessary labor and hence exploitation do not take place.[36] This does not in any way make this form of exploitation seem less bad. Not only are the patients in question exploited, they are deluded with respect to this fact. This seems to involve the infantilization Raz and Blake believe sticks to coercion. The upshot, as above, is that indirect or mediate coercion is at least as bad as direct coercion is from the point of autonomy.

Before proceeding I should note that Blake in fact leaves the option open that some types of justification, including coercion in the international sphere, are simply indefensible. Note, however, that if he were to claim this with respect to coercion in the international sphere then the disanalogy thesis to the effect that principles of equality or priority obtain, and only obtain, domestically, while only sufficitarian principles obtain globally would seem to collapse. It would so in the sense that domestic coercion is plausibly tied up with the structures of sovereignty, a crucial aspect of which is the ability to control membership. Hence, if the latter falls, that is, if it cannot be justified, then the former seems indefensible as well. Thus neither international nor domestic coercive structures would, on Blake's autonomy account, appear defensible, which would seem a rather bizarre implication.

To avoid such implications we may turn to a fourth suggestion as to how the directness or immediate thesis may be defended. The former suggestions, we may say, all point to cases in which we admittedly, from the point of view of autonomy, see something equally bad in indirect or mediate coercion. This, however, does not seem to exhaust the relevant cases. We may point to cases in which directness seems to matter in such a way that it makes the ongoing coercion more problematic than indirect coercion. To see this consider a version of Parfit's Bridge case.[37] Contemplate the difference (if any) between the case in which I, for no other reason than wanting to get rid of you, by my own force push you from a bridge just in time to make sure that you are run over by the oncoming train; and the case in which I for similar reasons by remote control release the trap-door you are standing on so that you with equal efficiency are run over by the train. Would this make a moral difference? In particular, does it suggest that the direct pushing is morally worse than the release of the trap-door? I think not. In both cases the end of all autonomous pursuits for you is just around the corner. From the point of view of autonomy this consequence of coercion whether direct or indirect is what fundamentally matters and hence I would tend to say that the two situations seem morally analogous. In the direct case the patient is of course in a vivid way confronted with an instance of autonomy-infringing coercion. All his autonomous pursuits are literally in the hands of the coercer. Still, it seems to me just as bad from the point of autonomy to pass away through some apparently impersonal force which is in fact authored by another agent. This would seem to take away in a morally relevant way the autonomous and conscious authorship of my life regarding a perhaps crucial part of this life, namely its ending, and to place it in the hands of another.[38] Thus I suggest again that we are left with no convincing argument to the effect that the direct coercion of state institutions (if indeed more direct than international coercion) is morally worse than the indirect coercion exercised by international institutions.

The paradoxical nature of state coercion

Blake alludes, as noted above, to reasons other than directness or immediateness for claiming a disanalogy between domestic and international spheres with respect to relevant principles of justice. One such other reason is the claim that state coercion is unique in virtue of its paradoxical nature, to wit, that it infringes autonomy and at the same time establishes crucial preconditions for autonomy.[39] With regard to the latter Blake refers to a familiar claim regarding rules, for example rules of property, namely their provision for security or stable expectations regarding the behavior of others.[40] The citizen of a given state, the reasonable thought seems to be, depends more on the domestic structures that apply to him, including the protection against external interventions and the protection against the unlawful actions of fellow citizens, for his autonomy than on international institutions in more or less their present form. I must admit that I find this suggested reason for claiming a disanalogy between coercive institutions with respect to justification and appropriate distributive principles peculiar. If a set of institutions in some sense infringes autonomy, and does not in another establish preconditions for autonomy, then relative to a set of institutions with the paradoxical nature of both infringing and providing necessary conditions for autonomy, this set seems a fortiori to stand in need of universally acceptable justification (which plausibly requires an impartial procedure which is likely to give rise to egalitarian or prioritarian principles). Furthermore, international coercion may in fact be just such a non-paradoxical set. As of yet we have been given no convincing reasons to believe that the effects on individual life chances of such institutions are less profound than the effects of domestic institutions, neither for holding that they coerce individuals less directly than domestic institutions or that if they did it would matter morally. In conjunction with the claim above that domestic institutions, as opposed to international ones, establish necessary conditions for autonomy, the upshot is that international institutions plausibly are institutions of the mentioned non-paradoxical nature with respect to which egalitarian or prioritarian principles of justice appear at least as relevant as they are with respect to domestic institutions.

If, in contrast, a set of institutions does not infringe autonomy, but establishes preconditions for autonomy, then it is unclear that it would stand in need of justification at all; it would in some sense seem self-justifying. It would be so in that it produces clear goods to those to whom it applies. Of course it is controversial that this suffices to justify an institution so perhaps we should make the less controversial claim, equally relevant in the present context, namely that providing for circumstances for autonomy does not appear urgently to call for justification.

So it is unclear why Blake believes that the claimed paradoxical nature of state coercion makes a justification by appeal to egalitarian or prioritarian principles especially relevant. Notably, the case of international coercion seems to need such justification much more pressingly. In terms of the Melilla case we may say that the African immigrants facing coercion with profound impact on their life chances, impacts we have not been given reasons not to believe infringe autonomy, seem to have a reasonable claim for a justification; a claim that seems more urgent than the claim for justification held by citizens who after all enjoy the autonomy-enhancing aspects of domestic coercion.

The autonomy-infringing nature of domestic coercion

I now turn to a further potential ground for Blake's disanalogy claim. Whereas this is not explicitly mentioned by Blake himself, it may arguably be seen as flowing from his commitment to autonomy and may have some appeal. The point may already have occurred to some readers when contemplating particular versions of direct and indirect coercion above. Recall that the paradigm case of autonomy-infringing coercion, according to Blake, is the case in which the will of one person is subsumed to that of another with the accompanying symbolic repercussions (infantilization and disrespect). I tried to illustrate this in a dramatic way with a version of the Bridge case. So the paradigm case is characterized by one person intentionally and deliberately making another act in a certain way—the way intended by the coercer. Now consider two of the cases considered when scrutinizing the direct-indirect distinction. I have in mind the case of women acting in certain ways that accord with chauvinist standards because they themselves partly accept the standards or cannot completely repudiate them, and the case of capitalist exploitation as opposed to feudal exploitation in which exploitation is an aspect of a complex institutional and impersonal relationship. While these cases plausibly involve concerns of relevance to autonomy—for example, the standards or structures may leave some agents with a set of options that is inadequate in the sense that it does not allow the individual to live an autonomous life—they might be thought not to involve the core concern of autonomy and accordingly do not call for justification of the kind appropriate for genuine autonomy-infringing acts and institutions. What is lacking for these cases to raise the core autonomy concern is an agent who deliberately and intentionally subsumes the will of another to his. The practices in question may work to the advantage of males and capitalists respectively and they may indeed individually and collectively play some role in upholding these practices and hence may to some extent be held responsible for the disadvantages they involve for women and workers respectively, but no one in particular and with evident intention restricts the options of women and workers in such a way that certain choices appear the best to them, namely those choices corresponding to the will of such an agent (if he indeed were present).

The autonomy theorist may then reason by analogy to the case of international coercion—immigration policies, for example. While they certainly affect the life chances of individuals, these effects may not be the intentional result of the actions of states. That is, each state individually may only intend that it should not admit a given poor immigrant, not that other states should not admit the immigrant. Hence, while other states may act on equally restrictive immigration laws implying that the poor immigrant has nowhere else to go, we do not have a case in which someone's options (the immigrant's) are deliberately and intentionally restricted in accordance with the will of another. Thus we have no clear infringement of autonomy and hence no call for a justification appealing to distributive shares arises.[41]

I begin the assessment of this suggested ground for Blake's disanalogy claim by noting that the implied absence of intentionality with regard to international coercive institutions such as immigration policies is doubtful at least. A number of informal and formal norms directing the admittance of immigrants to rich countries are upheld by the latter countries, most explicitly in the EU. Furthermore, it does not seem unfair to say that these norms tend towards a restrictive stance. Hence it is far from clear that the fact that staying home often seems the best option for poor immigrants is not a fact in virtue of a restrictive policy of immigration pursued jointly and intentionally by affluent countries. Accordingly, justification of a type comparable to the domestic case, that is an equalizing-implicating one, seems appropriate.

Let us grant, however, at least for the sake of argument, that international coercion in terms of immigration policies and its effects on potential immigrants is unintentional while domestic coercion, for example penal codes and tax policies, is indeed intentional. Is this, finally, a plausible ground on which one may rest the distinction between domestic and international coercion in such a way that the former, but not the latter, calls for justification by appeal to egalitarian or prioritarian principles? I am skeptical about this suggestion. I admit that the cases of sexist norms and capitalist exploitation, and by analogy, the case of international coercion, may not, due to the absence of a recognizable agent with evident intention, raise core concerns of autonomy.

Furthermore, I admit that cases like covert coercion in the Great Expectations case (which, I presume, would not be counted out by the autonomy theorist if intention is emphasized) suggest something of particular moral disvalue in cases where people face restrictive options (and even, as pointed out above, in cases where the option set of the agent expands in virtue of the agency of another). This goes as well for institutional orders in which the intentional restriction of people's options is predominant: these might be considered particularly bad in virtue of the clear attitude of autonomy-infringing disrespect they reflect.[42] I fail to see, however, that institutions not infringing autonomy in this way stand in no need of justification by appeal to egalitarian or prioritarian principles. This is especially the case when these institutions foreseeably and avoidably engender[43] restrictions of individuals' options; and that they do so is not denied by the proposal under consideration here. Market-inequalities are arguably not officially mandated or intentionally produced, but under realistic circumstances such are certainly generated (i.e. they are the foreseeable and avoidable upshot of an unregulated market) and domestically the pedigree of these inequalities does not mean that those attracted by the idea that there is a presumption against arbitrary inequalities recoil from saying that inequalities in these shares should be justified in virtue of being beneficial to the worst off.

The claims regarding respectively intentional autonomy-infringing and non-intentional non-autonomy-infringing restrictions on the options of individuals—both types of restrictions having profound effects on the life chances of individuals—are claims regarding the moral wrongness of such restrictions. I claimed that although intentional autonomy-infringing restrictions have a particular moral disvalue, which non-intentional non-autonomy-infringing restrictions do not share, the latter arguably still have a moral disvalue which makes justification by appeal to distributive shares appropriate. However, these claims leave the question of blame.[44] To this I will say that it is perfectly possible, indeed plausible, and of no consequence to my argument about moral wrongness and justification, that blame attaches more naturally and appropriately to intentional autonomy-infringing acts and institutions than to non-intentional non-autonomy-infringing acts and institutions. That is, if immigration policies of affluent states have profound but unintentional consequences for immigrants (in the sense that it is not intended by individual states that the only option of immigrants is to go back to their poor country of origin), then the policies may be morally wrong, but individual states may not be as blamable in this regard as they are with respect to the coercion of their own citizens. I stress that this assessment is a relative one suggesting that states may not be as blamable with respect to international coercion. They are not free from blame in that they play a role in upholding structures that profoundly harm individuals.

Conclusion

The proponents of the argument for the restricted writ of the moral presumption against arbitrary inequalities point to a number of properties in virtue of which they believe the legally coercive structure of the state is morally distinct, to wit: (i) domestic structures impose coercion in the name of its subjects, and they are asked to accept this coercion on moral grounds; (ii) domestic coercion is profound; (iii) domestic coercion is direct or immediate; (iv) domestic coercion is paradoxical in the sense that it infringes, but at the same time is a precondition for individual autonomy; (v) and/or domestic coercion is autonomy-infringing. I argued that (ii), (iii) and (v) are plausibly properties which are shared by international coercive structures such as immigration policies and analogously calling for justification by reference to principles of justice. Furthermore, even assuming that (iii) and (v) are unique to domestic institutions would not imply that principles are only relevant at the domestic level. In so far as the coercion takes place through no choice or fault of the affected individuals and that the coercion is profound (cf. ii), the strength of the reasons for redistribution with a neutralizing tendency is unaltered. Finally, (i) and (iv) if true of domestic institution, and not of international institutions, which plausibly is the case, appear if anything to make principles of justice more relevant at the international level than at the domestic level. The upshot is that the proposed grounds for the asserted disanalogy between domestic and international institutions such that egalitarian or prioritarian principles obtain in the former but not in the latter are unconvincing.

Notes

* For pertinent comments I am grateful to the editor, an anonymous reviewer, the members of the section for Political Theory, Department of Political Science, University of Aarhus, participants at the conference "Ethical responsibility in relations between communities and states" arranged by *The Centre for the Study of Mind in Nature,* November 6–7, 2008, University of Oslo, and participants in the annual meeting of the Danish Philosophical Association in Aarhus 2009. I am especially grateful to Chris Armstrong, Nils Holtug, Sune Lægaard, Kasper Lippert-Ramussen, and Andrew Williams.

1 Rawls (1971, 18, 72; 1999, 16, 62–63). Cf. Nagel (1979, 118). See also Barry (1989, 213–15).
2 See, for example, Amdur (1977, 453–54 and the references he provides); Barry (1978, 238; 1989, 183–90); Beitz (1979, 136–43; 1983, 593); Richards (1982, 289–90).
3 See, for example, Caney (2001, 125; 2005, 111–12; 2008, 505–6); Moellendorf (2002, 55–56, 79); Pogge (1989, 247; 1994, 198); Tan (2004, 27–28, 159–60).
4 Caney (2008, 505).
5 Cf. Cohen (1997, 18).
6 Which inequalities (if any) benefit the worst off is, of course, controversial. See Cohen (2008, esp. chap. 1–3). This is not, however, important to the argument pursued here.
7 Blake (2001); Nagel (2005). For related arguments see Miller (1998); Risse (2006, 671–98); Sangiovanni (2007).
8 Nagel (2005, 128–29); Cf. Rawls 1971, 7, 343–344; 1999, 7, 302). Cf. Rawls (1993, 136).
9 Nagel (2005, 128–29). Cf. Rawls (1993, 67–68, cf. 135–36). See also Blake (2001, sec. V).
10 See, for example, Cohen (1986; 1994, 1531ff.); Dent (1988, 171); Kant (1993, 38 [431]).
11 Blake (2001, 282–83); Nagel (1979, 119; 1991, 33–34; 2005, 129). Cf. Ronald Dworkin's argument to the effect that the justification of state coercion is dependent upon the state showing equal concern and respect for its citizens. According to Dworkin, this means adopting a resourcist egalitarian conception which neutralizes inequalities pertaining to people's circumstances (that is, undeserved or non-culpable inequalities). See Dworkin (1986, chap. 6, esp. 190–215; 2000, 1–2). Andrew Williams drew my attention to the pedigree of the argument under consideration.
12 Nagel (2005, 129–30).
13 Cf. Caney (2008, 487–518, esp. "A Theoretical Framework," 488–91 on different versions of disanalogy arguments.
14 Miller (2007, "introduction").
15 Cohen (1997, 28).
16 It is crucial to note, as will be clear below, that my point against Nagel is not that arbitrary inequalities obtain globally as well. Nagel accepts that fact, but submits that it is only in

the domestic sphere that such inequalities stand in need of justification. My point is that when individuals, without being given a choice, are subject to coercive institutions which allow arbitrary differences this suffices for a justificatory burden to arise—a burden which can only be lifted by appeal to principles of equality or priority. That is, I deny, pace Nagel, that the questions whether people coerced in this way may regard the coercion as being imposed in their name and whether they are asked to accept it (questions which we may plausibly answer affirmatively in the domestic case, but not in the global case) are morally relevant in a sense which makes calls for justification appropriate only in the case that the question are answered affirmatively.

17 Cf. Abizadeh (2008).
18 I owe this point to an anonymous reviewer. It is also an important strategy of argument in Pogge (2002). Pogge points to patterns of inequality and partiality in the domestic case which we would never regard as just and ask why similar or worse patterns are not regarded as equally unjust (see, esp. chap. 3–5).
19 Cf. the point that A. J. Julius makes in his criticism of Nagel in (Julius 2006, 180).
20 Blake (2001, 267).
21 Raz (1986).
22 Blake (2001, 267).
23 Blake (2001, 270, 272).
24 Blake (2001, 268). See, further, pp. 270, 272.
25 Blake (2001, 270). The case in which a person makes an action costly to another may plausibly fall under this notion of autonomy. For the distinction between something being difficult and something being costly, see Cohen (2000 [1978], 238–39). By making alternative options difficult, impossible or costly we may say that the coercer leaves the person he coerces with inadequate or unreasonable alternatives. See Cohen (1988, 245).
26 Blake (2001, 272–77).
27 Blake (2003, 228).
28 David Miller makes similar claims in Miller (2010).
29 I discuss Blake's account for the profoundness of domestic coercion under the assumption that the notion of profoundness at issue is related to Rawls's reason for focusing on the basic structure—that "its effects are so profound and present from the start" (Rawls 1971, 7; 1999, 7). Cf. Abizadeh (2007, 343–45). Note that Nagel does not, as mentioned above in the text, rely on the profoundness case for a disanalogy, in fact, he emphasizes the material effects of immigration policies (Nagel 2005, 129–30).
30 Cf. Risse (2006, 684ff.).
31 Blake (2001, 280, cf. p. 265. Italics added).
32 Blake (2001, 272).

33 Blake (2001, 273–77, and the quote above in the text).
34 Cf. Marx (1997, 69).
35 In this case, as in others mentioned above, there is no agent intentionally molding the option set of another, and this may be crucial for the question of autonomy. I return to this proposition below.
36 Cohen (2000 [1978], chap. V); Rawls (2007).
37 Parfit (2002; 2011, 218).
38 Cf. Dworkin (1993, 199).
39 Blake (2001, 265, 280–82).
40 Blake (2001, 280).
41 The suggested position is inspired by Miller's observations in (2010).
42 Cf. Pogge (2002, 41–42).
43 Cf. Pogge (2002, 41–42) and (1989, chap. 1).
44 Cf. Cohen (1997, sec. VI).

References

Abizadeh, Arash (2007). "Cooperation, Pervasive Impact, and Coercion: On the Scope (not Site) of Distributive Justice." *Philosophy & Public Affairs* 35, no. 4: 343–45.

Abizadeh, Arash (2008). "Democratic Theory and Border Coercion: No Right to Unilaterally Control Your Own Borders." *Political Theory* 36: 37–65.

Amdur, Robert (1977). "Rawls's Theory of Justice: Domestic and International Perspectives." *World Politics* 29, no. 3: 438–61.

Barry, Brian (1978). "Circumstances of Justice and Future Generations." In R. Sikora and Brian Barry (eds.), *Obligations to Future Generations*. Temple University Press.

Barry, Brian (1989). *Theories of Justice: A Treatise on Social Justice*, vol. 1. Berkeley, CA: University of California Press.

Beitz, Charles (1979). *Political Theory and International Relations*. Princeton University Press.

Beitz, Charles (1983). "Cosmopolitan Ideals and National Sentiment." *The Journal of Philosophy* 80, no. 10: 591–600.

Blake, Michael (2001). "Distributive Justice, State Coercion, and Autonomy." *Philosophy & Public Affairs* 30, no. 3: 257–96

Blake, Michael (2003). "Immigration." In R. G. Frey and Christopher Heath Wellman (eds.), *A Companion to Applied Ethics*. Malden, Oxford and Carlton: Blackwell.

Caney, Simon (2001). "Cosmopolitan Justice and Equalizing Opportunities." In T. Pogge (ed.), Global Justice. Oxford: Blackwell.

Caney, Simon (2005). *Justice Beyond Borders:* A Global Political Theory. Oxford: Oxford University Press.

Caney, Simon (2008). "Global Distributive Justice and the State." *Political Studies* 56: 487–518.

Cohen, G. A. (1988). *History, Labour, and Freedom.* Oxford: Clarendon Press.

Cohen, G. A. (1997). "Where the Action Is: On the Site of Distributive Justice." *Philosophy & Public Affairs* 26, no. 1: 3–30.

Cohen, G. A. (2000). *Karl Marx's Theory of History:* A Defence. Oxford: Clarendon Press.

Cohen, G. A. (2008 [1978]). *Rescuing Justice & Equality.* Cambridge, Massachusetts, London: Harvard University Press.

Cohen, Joshua (1986). "Reflections on Rousseau: Autonomy and Democracy." *Philosophy & Public Affairs* 15: 257–97.

Cohen, Joshua (1994). "A More Democratic Liberalism." *Michigan Law Review* 92: 1503–46.

Dent, N. J. H (1988). *Rousseau—An Introduction to his Psychological, Social and Political Theory.* Oxford and NY: Basil Blackwell.

Dworkin, Ronald (1986). *Law's Empire.* London: Fontana Press.

Dworkin (1993). *Life's Dominion:* An Argument about Abortion, Euthanasia, and Individual Freedom. New York: Vintage Books.

Dworkin, Ronald (2000). *Sovereign Virtue: The Theory and Practice of Equality.* Cambridge MA and London: Harvard University Press.

Julius, A. J. (2006). "Nagel's Atlas." *Philosophy & Public Affairs* 34, no. 2: 176–92.

Kent, Immanuel (1993). *Grounding for the Metaphysics of Morals with "On a Supposed Right to Lie because of Philanthropic Concerns.* Indianapolis and Cambridge: Hackett Publishing Company.

Marx, Karl (1997). "Towards a Critique of Hegel's *Philosophy of Right:* Introduction." In David McLellan (ed.), *Karl Marx: Selected Writings.* Oxford: Oxford University Press.

Miller, Richard W. (1998). "Cosmopolitan Respect and Patriotic Concern." *Philosophy & Public Affairs* 27, no. 3: 202–24.

Miller (2007). *National Responsibility and Global Justice.* Oxford: Oxford University Press.

Miller, David (2010). "Why Immigration Controls Are Not Coercive: A Reply to Arash Abizadeh." *Political Theory* 38, no. 1: 111–20.

Moellendorf, D (2002). *Cosmopolitan Justice.* Boulder, CO: Westview Press.

Nagel, Thomas (1979). *Mortal Questions.* Cambridge: Cambridge University Press.

Nagel, Thomas (1991). *Equality and Partiality.* NY and Oxford: Oxford University Press.

Nagel, Thomas (2005). "The Problem of Global Justice." *Philosophy & Public Affairs* 30, no. 2: 113–47.

Parfit, Derek (2002). *What We Could Rationally Will.* The Tanner Lectures on Human Values delivered at University of California at Berkeley delivered at University of California at Berkeley November 4, 5, and 6, 2002, p. 299/15, http://www.tannerlectures.utah.edu/lectures/documents/volume24/parfit_2002.pdf

Parfit, Derek (2011). *On What Matters,* vol. 1. Oxford: Oxford University Press.

Pogge, Thomas (1989). *Realizing Rawls.* Ithaca, NY: Cornell University Press.

Pogge, Thomas (1994). "An Egalitarian Law of People." *Philosophy & Public Affairs* 23, no. 2: 195–224.

Pogge, Thomas (2002). *World Poverty and Human Rights.* Cambridge, UK, and Malden, MA: Polity.

Rawls, John (1971). *A Theory of Justice.* Cambridge, MA: The Belknap Press of Harvard University Press.

Rawls, John (1993). *Liberalism.* New York: Columbia University Press.

Rawls, John (1999). *A Theory of Justice,* rev. edition. Oxford: Oxford University Press.

Rawls, John (2007). "Lectures on Marx." *Lectures on the Historical of Political Philosphy.* Harvard University Press.

Raz, Joseph (1986). T*he Morality of Freedom.* Oxford: Clarendon Press

Richards, David A. J. (1982). "International Distributive Justice." In J. Roland Pennock and John W. Chapman, *Ethics, Economics, and the Law.* New York: New York University Press.

Risse, Mathias (2006). "What to Say About the State." *Social Theory and Practice* 32, no. 4: 671–98.

Sangiovanni, Andrea (2007). "Global Justice, Reciprocity, and the State." *Philosophy & Public Affairs* 35, no. 13–39.

Tan, K. C. (2004). *Justice without Borders: Cosmopolitanism, Nationalism and Patriotism.* Cambridge: Cambridge University Press.

CONCEPTUAL FOUNDATIONS OF OPERATIONAL SET THEORY

KAJ BØRGE HANSEN

Uppsala University

Abstract

I formulate the Zermelo-Russell paradox for naive set theory. A sketch is given of Zermelo's solution to the paradox: the cumulative type structure. A careful analysis of the set formation process shows a missing component in this solution: the necessity of an assumed imaginary jump out of an infinite universe. Thus a set is formed by a suitable combination of concrete and imaginary operations all of which can be made or assumed by a Turing machine. Some consequences are drawn from this improved analysis of the concept of set, for the theory of sets and for the philosophy and foundations of mathematics.

1 **Cantorian Sets**. Cantor defined in 1895 a set as "any collection of definite, distinguishable objects of our intuition or of our intellect to be conceived as a whole." This is the conceptual basis of the so-called naive set theory, and it leads directly to contradictions.

2 **Russell's Paradox**. We operate in the domain V of all sets. Let r be the collection of all sets which are not members of themselves:
(2-1) $r = \{x \mid x \notin x\}$
r is clearly a set according to Cantor's definition. It is therefore meaningful to ask whether $r \in r$. By the Principle of Extensionality,
(2-2) $r \in r \Leftrightarrow r \notin r$
which is a contradiction.

3 REMARK. The paradox was discovered independently by Bertrand Russell and by Ernst Zermelo at the beginning of the twentieth century. The two men suggested solutions to the paradox based on the idea that the set universe is organised in types. Russell based his Theory of Types explicitly

on this idea. Zermelo developed his own version of the idea into the *cumulative type structure* and based axiomatic set theory on it. His set theory *Z* was later amended by Skolem and Fraenkel and by von Neumann and Zermelo himself into Zermelo-Fraenkel set theory *ZF*. Here I consider only the cumulative type structure and ZF for the following reasons: (1) ZF is still the most widely used set theory while the Theory of Types is mostly of historical interest. (2) The cumulative type structure is more general than the type structure of the Simple Type Theory; the simple types are all present in it. Moreover, the Ramified Theory of Types has a model in ZF. I base the analysis on the expositions in Drake (1974) and Shoenfield (1977) which are more up to date than Zermelo's own account.

4 **Cumulative Type Structure**. The sets are organised in levels (or types):
  Level 0: A collection of individuals (called atoms)
  Level 1: All collections whose members are individuals of Level 0.
  Level 2: All collections whose members are in Level 0 or 1.
  . . . .
  Level α: All collections whose members are in earlier levels.
  . . . .

In standard ZF, it is assumed that we have no atoms so that Level 0 is empty. The sequence of levels is assumed to have no conceivable end. Thus it is supposed that there are infinite sets and hence levels infinitely high in the hierarchy.

5 **V-hierarchy**. Once the axioms of ZFC, ZF with the Axiom of Choice, have been formulated based on the intuition of the cumulative type structure, we can define the V-hierarchy which essentially reconstructs the cumulative type structure in ZFC:

(5-1) $V_0 = \emptyset$
  $V_{\alpha+1} = P(V_\alpha)$
  $V_\alpha = \cup_{\beta < \alpha} V_\beta$ if α is a limit ordinal
  $V = \cup_{On(\alpha)} V_\alpha$

The indices are ordinals. 'On(α)' means that α is an ordinal. If X is a set, $P(X)$ is the set of all subsets of X, the power set of X. The V_α are sets, while

V is a proper class and contains all sets. Let a be an arbitrary set. By the *type* of a, we understand the smallest ordinal α such that $a \in V_\alpha$. Non-empty sets have other sets as members. Sets can be members of other sets and of proper classes. Proper classes can be members of neither sets nor proper classes. This gives the solution in the cumulative type structure to Russell's paradox. By the Axiom of Foundation, Russell's class $r = V$ so that r is a proper class. Then we cannot even ask whether $r \in r$. Alternatively: If r had been a set, it should have some type $\alpha+1$. Then all elements of r must be of type α or lower. As a matter of fact, no set in the Cumulative Type Structure can contain itself. Therefore r must contain all sets, including all sets of types bigger than α. Then r must both contain and not contain sets of types bigger than α. Therefore r is not a set. It is not obvious from the outset that the types should be as many as (5-1) indicates, one for every ordinal number. However, some of the properties we want the set universe to satisfy force this structure upon us. Thus the Axiom of Infinity together with the Power Set Axiom demand the existence of V_ω, $V_{\omega+1}$, $V_{\omega+2}$, ..., and the Axiom of Replacement demands the existence of $V_{\omega+\omega}$ and all the V_α beyond $V_{\omega+\omega}$.

6 QUOTATION. Shoenfield has some interesting formulations in his account of the cumulative type structure: "The explanation [of Russell's paradox] is not really difficult. When we are forming a set z by choosing its members, we do not yet have the object z, and hence cannot use it as a member of z. The same reasoning shows that certain other sets cannot be members of z. For example, suppose that $z \in y$. Then we cannot form y until we have formed z. Hence y is not available as an object when z is formed, and therefore cannot be a member of z. (...) Carrying the analysis a bit further, we arrive at the following. Sets are formed in *stages*. For each stage S, there are certain stages which are *before* S. At stage S, each collection consisting of sets formed at stages before S is formed into a set. There are no sets other than the sets which are formed at the stages. (...) Thus the fundamental question for us is: given a collection **S** of stages, is there a stage after all the members of **S**? (...) [T]he answer to our question cannot always be yes. For example, if **S** is the collection of all stages, then there is no stage after every stage in **S**."

7 ANALYSIS. (I) The present analysis is based on the view that the cumulative type structure mainly is a sound approach to the solution of the paradox-

es of naive set theory, in particular Russell's paradox. Nevertheless there are problems surrounding the definition of the cumulative type structure which need to be addressed.

(II) Shoenfield's stages, the levels of the cumulative type structure, and the types of the V-hierarchy are the same. There is, however, an important difference between his exposition and Drake's exposition in §4. In the latter (which is close to Zermelo's original version), it apparently is suggested that the sets of the set universe exist in themselves and just happen to be organised in levels. In Shoenfield's version, the sets and the levels are the results of a *formation process*. I sympathise with Shoenfield's account because it explains where the levels come from. It also implies that the sets do not exist in themselves but are the results of a kind of idealised mental construction process. This leads, however, to a new problem which Shoenfield seems not to have noticed himself. Since sets are the results of a formation process, they are formed by *operations* which human beings can do in principle, i.e., disregarding the fact that we have only a finite memory at our disposal. For all we know, all operations we can do are such operations which can be performed by a Turing machine. Therefore the right way to study the properties of sets is to study set forming operations which can be performed by a Turing machine. The axioms of ZFC state that certain sets exist, for instance infinite sets, power sets of infinite sets, and choice sets. If these axioms are taken literally, they are simply false because sets do not exist in themselves. If they should not be taken literally, we need to know what they really stand for instead and then replace the existence axioms by assumptions which explicitly state what is behind the existence axioms. The claim in the present paper is that the existence axioms of ZFC and other set theories are better replaced by assumptions on operations.

(III) Zermelo's, Drake's, and Shoenfield's conception of a set is still quite similar to Cantor's. They all see a set as a mere collection. If we look closer at the set formation process, we see that this is insufficient. A set can be a member of other sets and of proper classes. Therefore it must be conceived of as an object, that is, it must be *seen from the outside* as an individual in a universe larger than the set is in itself. The set formation process is determined by the definition of the V-hierarchy together with axioms which postulate the existence of certain subsets of the V_α. For finite sets, it can be considered trivial that a Turing machine can perform an object forming operation by taking the members of the set together and treat the collection as one object. Therefore all V_n and their elements can be considered sets. The formation of a finite set is a *real operation* which can be performed by a universal Turing machine. Now consider the infinite set V_ω which contains precisely the hereditarily finite sets as members. From the definition of the V-hierarchy, we can see how V_ω is formed. First we take the union of the finite V_n, $V_\omega = \cup_n V_n$. This gives us V_ω as a class or collection: the universe of all hereditarily finite sets. So far we can only see V_ω from the inside as a universe. To get V_ω as a set, we need to make a jump out of the universe V_ω and see it from the outside. Since V_ω is infinite, we cannot really make the jump and neither can a universal Turing machine. We must assume the jump made, and then consider the consequences of such an assumption. This kind of formation process consists of a combination of recursive set forming operations and an *assumption* about a jump having been made (though it really cannot be done). We call this an *imaginary operation*. We may compare with the proper class $V = \cup_{On(\alpha)} V_\alpha$ where $On(\alpha)$ means that α is an ordinal. It is the universe of all sets. It cannot, given the premises of the cumulative type structure, be seen from the outside as an object. We cannot progress further beyond collecting all sets into a universe by assuming a jump made out of V because V occurs after all the formation stages and therefore after all possible imaginary jumps considered admissible in set theory already have been made.

(IV) From the definition of the V-hierarchy, we can see what set formation operations, real or imaginary, we need. First we form the empty set out of nothing, $V_0 = \emptyset$. Then we form all hereditarily finite sets by $V_{n+1} = P(V_n)$, n = 0, 1, 2, ... All hereditarily finite sets can be constructed recursively. Now consider infinite sets V_α where α is a limit ordinal. Assume all V_β, $\beta < \alpha$, have been formed as sets. Then V_α is formed as a set as follows. First we collect all sets in the V_β to a universe by taking the union $V_\alpha = \cup_{\beta<\alpha} V_\beta$. Next we get V_α as an object and hence a set by assuming a jump out of the universe V_α. Since such a jump cannot really be done, it is a non-constructive operation. When $\alpha = \beta+1$ is a successor ordinal, we proceed as follows to obtain V_α. Assume that V_β has been formed as a set. First we form the universe of all subsets of V_β. This is a partly non-constructive process. In the case of $V_\beta = V_\omega$, $P(V_\beta)$ can, as a potential infinity, be formed in a recursive process by using a binary tree, constructing it step by step from the root node and upwards in the tree.

So far every branch and the tree as a whole represent only universes, that is, potential infinities. First we must close each of the branches into a set. For each branch, this involves only one imaginary jump but no jump, real or imaginary, beyond the type of jump needed to make V_ω a set. A new imaginary operation is needed, though, because the operation must be assumed to be made 2^ω times. Now we have $P(V_\omega)$ as a universe of subsets of V_ω. To get $P(V_\omega)$ as a set, we must assume an imaginary jump made out of the universe $P(V_\omega)$, or alternatively out of the universe of branches of the binary tree. In the case of $\beta > \omega$, $P(V_\beta)$ can, as a universe, be formed by using a transfinite binary tree T. If γ is the cardinality of V_β, the depth of T is γ. The subsets of V_β are determined by the branches of T. We then proceed essentially as in the case of $P(V_\omega)$ to get first $V_{\beta+1} = P(V_\beta)$ as a universe of the subsets of V_β and then, by an imaginary jump out of this universe, $P(V_\beta)$ as a set. The existence axioms of ZFC can then be seen to be true in the cumulative type structure (or the V-hierarchy).

(V) To sum up: Sets do not exist in themselves. Instead they are the results of a formation process. This process consists of operations, real and imaginary, which (in principle) can be made or, in the mind, assumed made. We have found that there are at least three types of such set forming operations:

(1) *Real operations* which are finite recursive operations that can be performed by a universal Turing machine.

(2) Given an infinite set M, the *imaginary operation* consisting in the *formation of the uncountable universe* containing all the $2^{|M|}$ subsets of M. (An imaginary operation is a combination of a real operation with an assumption about the performance of an operation which cannot really be done.) This can be done by using for instance a transfinite binary tree of depth α where α is the cardinality of M.

(3) Given an infinite universe M seen from the inside, the *imaginary operation* of assuming a jump from inside the universe M and out of M so that M, after the *imaginary jump out of the universe*, is seen from the outside as an object in a larger universe and hence as a set. This kind of imaginary jump out of a universe is well known to almost every child after the age of 2-3 years and to almost every grown-up person. It is the imaginary jump out of oneself which the child makes when he (or she) becomes self-conscious. He reaches the stage of development where he adopts the hypothesis that he is only one individual among several others, that his inner world is not

identical with the whole world but has counterparts in other similar human individuals, and that there outside him is a bigger world in which he is only one among many other individuals.

8 REMARK. Though the observations in the analysis are simple, they turn out to have dramatic consequences. A few will be considered here.

9 **Axiomatic Method**. After Zermelo's work, it has been an unquestioned dogma among set theorists that axiomatic set theory is the only acceptable way of developing theories of sets. If the set universe had existed ready-made, this should be a justifiable point of view. But sets do not exist in themselves; they are the results of a formation process consisting of real and imaginary operations. In contrast to sets, operations do exist in the physical world. Then their mathematical counterparts, operations by the universal Turing machine and recursive functions, can also be assumed to exist. From this point of view, the right way of developing a theory of sets is to take a mathematical theory of computations and recursive functions as starting point and study the set formation process: the set forming real operations performed by Turing machines and the interplay between real operations and assumptions in imaginary set forming operations. Thus such a theory of real and imaginary operations is the proper foundations of set theory. Derive from these foundations what sets there can be and which properties they have! I call this procedure *operational set theory* and contrast it with axiomatic set theory. I claim that operational set theory, rather than the theory of types and axiomatic set theory, is the right solution to the set paradoxes. The axiomatic approach to set theory and mathematics in general is not the only possible approach, and sometimes it is not the best approach either.

10 **Unsolved Problems**. (I) The most important contributions to set theory during the second half of the twentieth century are the discovery of forcing and Boolean-valued models and the proofs that some hitherto unsolved problems of set theory are unsolvable in the existing set theories like ZFC. Notable examples of unsolved problems are the Continuum Hypothesis, the Generalised Continuum Hypothesis, Souslin's problem, and the existence of large cardinals. This calls for the formulation of new axioms which can be seen to be true in the cumulative type structure and which imply solutions to

the unsolved problems. It has turned out to be unexpectedly difficult to find acceptable axioms and very little progress has been made during the last half-century. The suggestion here is that operational set theory might be helpful to provide progress towards a solution. The methods tried so far are based only on an intuitive understanding of the cumulative type structure. The contention is that a careful analysis of the set formation process, the real and imaginary operations which generate the sets, can produce sufficiently adequate and precise information about what sort of sets can exist and what properties they have and which sets cannot exist to allow a complete answer to the unsolved problems—or alternatively prove that they are unsolvable in an absolute sense. In operational set theory, we will no longer be handicapped by the vagueness hampering mere intuition. Moreover, the representation of operations by recursive functions might make it possible to apply the Church-Turing thesis in the solution of problems in operational set theory.

(II) As an example, we consider the Continuum Problem. By the relative consistency and independence results by Gödel and Cohen, the continuum problem is unsolvable in ZFC. Since the V-hierarchy is definable in ZFC and the V-hierarchy is a cumulative type structure according to the conditions given by Zermelo, the cumulative type structure *as defined* does not contain a solution to the continuum problem. To solve it, we need to develop the cumulative type structure further. This implies developing the concept of a set further. The program of operational set theory attempts to do just that. It might turn out that the continuum problem is solvable in operational set theory. If it does not turn out so, it might, on ontological grounds, be possible to argue convincingly that operational set theory is as far as it is possible to develop the concept of set. This might then be a way to show that the continuum problem is unsolvable in an absolute sense.

11 **Constructive Mathematics**. In the original version of intuitionism, Brouwer and Heyting succeeded well with the development of arithmetic. The attempts to develop analysis within the framework of classical intuitionism failed, however. Starting in the 1960s, E. Bishop (constructive analysis), P. Martin-Löf (intuitionistic type theory), and P. Aczel (constructive set theory) among others liberalised the framework of classical intuitionism in order to obtain a more adequate intuitionistic basis for modern mathematics, including mathematical analysis. They claim that this neo-intuitionistic pro-

gram still gives rise only to constructive mathematics. I now show that their claim is unwarranted.

(I) One kind of proof procedure which is said to be constructive in some forms of neo-intuitionism consists of proof by ordinal induction up to a suitable countable ordinal $>\omega$, for instance up to ε_0 as in Gentzen's proof of the consistency of Peano Arithmetic. As a simple example, we consider induction up to $\omega 2 = \omega+\omega$. The ordinal $\omega 2$ has the structure

$$\omega 2 = \omega+\omega = \{0, 1, 2, \ldots, \omega, \omega+1, \omega+2, \ldots\}$$

where $0 = \emptyset$, $n+1 = n \cup \{n\}$, $\omega = \{0, 1, 2, \ldots\}$, $\omega+n+1 = \omega+n \cup \{\omega+n\}$. Suppose we want to prove a sentence

(11-1) $\qquad \forall\alpha(\alpha < \omega 2 \to A(\alpha))$

by ordinal induction up to $\omega 2$. Then we must show

(11-2) $\qquad A(0)$
(11-3) $\qquad (\forall n\in \omega)(A(n) \to A(n+1))$
(11-4) $\qquad A(\omega)$
(11-5) $\qquad (\forall n\in \omega)(A(\omega+n) \to A(\omega+n+1))$

For the part of the proof which consists of induction up to ω and the conclusion $\forall n\, A(n)$, it suffices to consider ω a universe (a potential infinity). But for the rest of the proof, lines (11-4) and (11-5), we need ω as a set. In particular, the conclusion $A(\omega)$ demands that ω is a set. This, in turn, demands that we assume the existence of an imaginary jump out of the universe $\omega = \{0, 1, 2, \ldots\}$. Since such a jump cannot really be made, it is non-constructive. In other words, every inductive proof over the ordinals which goes beyond the natural numbers is non-constructive. To make the induction, we do not really need the ordinal $\omega+\omega$. We might instead for instance use the isomorphic structure

$$\{0, 2, 4, \ldots, 1, 3, 5, \ldots\}$$

Here 1 has the same place as ω. 1 is not, or need not be considered, a set. This makes no essential difference. In order to come to 1 in the inductive process, we *must* make an imaginary, and hence non-constructive, jump out of the universe $\{0, 2, 4, \ldots\}$. Neo-intuitionists claim that modern constructive mathematics has no problems with infinite sets. It (and the neo-intuitionists) ought to have. Every infinite set involves at least one imaginary jump out of a universe and therefore is non-constructive. Neo-intuitionists need not have problems with countably infinite classes. At least all recursively enumerable *classes* can be considered constructive. On the other hand, all infinite *sets*, whether recursively enumerable or not, are non-constructive. This kind of neo-intuitionists have liberalised intuitionistic mathematics into non-constructive mathematics.

(II) We now consider Per Martin-Löf's Intuitionistic Type Theory, MLTT, and Peter Aczel's Constructive Set Theory, CZF. CZF is essentially a reformulation of the set theory in MLTT in the language of classical set theory. The basic principle in MLTT and CZF is to allow as constructive sets all and only such classical sets which are recursively enumerable. CZF does not have the Power Set Axiom of ZF. It still has the Principle of Exponentiation:

(11-6)   If A is a CZF set, then so is $\{0, 1\}^A$.

It is understood that $\{0, 1\}^A$ contains only the recursive functions from A to $\{0, 1\}$. Let $A = \underline{N}$. Being recursive, it is a CZF set and we then get as a CZF set $\{0, 1\}^{\underline{N}}$ containing all recursive functions from $\underline{N}$ to $\{0, 1\}$. It is, of course, countable. On the other hand, the uncountable classical set $\{0, 1\}^{\underline{N}}$ is not a CZF set. The trouble for CZF and MLTT is that the classical $\{0, 1\}^{\underline{N}}$, as a potential infinity, seems to be constructive. Consider the complete binary tree. Label each edge towards the left from a node by 0 and each edge to the right from a node by 1. This labelled tree can be constructed by a recursive procedure which yields all the nodes and the tree structure and therefore also all the branches as a potential infinity. There are continuum many branches in the tree, and each branch is identical with a sequence in the classical $\{0, 1\}^{\underline{N}}$ and vice versa. Thus the tree is constructive and it is essentially identical with the classical class $\{0, 1\}^{\underline{N}}$ which in turn essentially is identical with the classical class $P(\underline{N})$. Therefore MLTT and CZF face the following dilemma. If they do not allow the classical $\{0, 1\}^{\underline{N}}$ and $P(\underline{N})$ as classes (CZF sets), then they are incomplete because, as classes, these entities are as constructive as $\underline{N}$. If they do allow the classical $\{0, 1\}^{\underline{N}}$ and $P(\underline{N})$ as classes (sets) in CZF, then CZF collapses as a constructive set theory and becomes non-constructive. It is instructive to compare with the recognised CZF set $\{0, 1\}^{\underline{N}}$. It contains all and only the recursive functions $f: \underline{N} \to \{0, 1\}$. They correspond to the countable set of branches in the binary tree which are recursively enumerable *separately*. Not all branches in the full binary tree are recursively enumerable separately; but all branches can be recursively enumerated in *parallel*. Therefore the full binary tree is a recursively enumerable structure and therefore the corresponding class $P(\underline{N})$ ought to be considered a legitimate MLTT and CZF set, it seems. My purpose here is, of course, not to show that the classical set $P(\underline{N})$ is a constructive set. In Analysis 7, I have showed that it is not. My purpose is to show that, based on the philosophical principles which Martin-Löf and Aczel take as conceptual foundations of MLTT and CZF, $P(\underline{N})$ ought to be included as a set in these theories.

(III) The situation is even worse. Since $\omega = \{0, 1, 2, \ldots\}$ is recursive, it is a CZF set. Then by Exponentiation (11-6), $\{0, 1\}^\omega$ is a CZF set. The members of $\{0, 1\}^\omega$ are all the recursive functions $f: \omega \to \{0, 1\}$. Let $K_\omega: \omega \to \{0, 1\}$ be the characteristic function for ω. Then K_ω is the constant function $K_\omega(n) = 1$ for all $n \in \omega$ so that K_ω is recursive and hence $K_\omega \in \{0, 1\}^\omega$. Since K_ω represents ω, this is equivalent with saying that $\omega \in \{0, 1\}^\omega$. Analysis 7 shows that assigning membership status to ω implies treating it as an object and that this cannot be done in a constructive way.

(IV) The operational point of view makes it fairly easy to discover non-constructive aspects of MLTT and CZF. To sum up: (1) Infinite collections like ω are in MLTT and CZF treated as objects. This implies treating them as classical sets which cannot be done constructively. (2) MLTT and CZF allows induction up to some countable ordinals larger than ω, for instance up to ε_0. Any such induction demands at least one non-constructive jump out of an infinite universe. (3) $P(\omega)$ can be represented by a binary tree. This tree in turn can, as a potential infinity, be defined by a recursive function. By Martin-Löf's own philosophical principle for admissible sets, the classical set $P(\omega)$ ought to be included in MLTT and CZF but is not.

12 Category Theory.

(I) Mathematicians study not only individual structures and their properties but also different classes of structures and how such classes are related to each other. Let, for instance, **G** be the class of all groups, and let V be the class of all sets. Since for every non-empty set G there is at least one group (G, *, e, $^{-1}$) having G as its basic set, **G** is a proper class. It is natural to consider for instance the mapping

$f: \mathbf{G} \to V$

which maps every group to its basic set:

(G, *, e, $^{-1}$) $\to$ G

In category theory, f is called the *stripping functor* because it strips the group of all structure and leaves only the naked set G. Since **G** and V are proper classes, they can be defined in NBG set theory; but there is no way to define f as a set or class. Nevertheless, f is a natural and useful mathematical object in the given context, and it does not seem to lead to contradictions to introduce such mappings. The solution, first suggested by Eilenberg and MacLane, is to introduce the concept of a category. A *category* is a collection of mappings, called *morphisms*. The idea is that the properties of objects like algebraic structures, topological spaces, sets, and classes can be defined in terms of properties of the morphisms which have the objects as domains or co-domains.

(II) Using such methods, we can also study sets and the set universe. One such theory is *CS*, the theory of the category of all sets. A more powerful alternative is *topos theory*. Both theories were created and developed by F. W. Lawvere, and topos theory also by M. Tierney. The basic idea is to look at sets and classes from the outside as *black boxes*. In physics, a black box is characterised by the *causal relations* it has to other objects. In mathematics, a black box is characterised by the *functional relations* it has to other mathematical objects. This is precisely how category theory works: Properties of the morphisms are used to define the inner properties of the sets and classes—including proper classes like V—which are domains or co-domains of the morphisms. There are some problems with the categorial approach to sets and classes.

(1) If sets had existed in themselves, the categorial way of defining the properties of sets and classes had been fully acceptable. As we have seen, sets are the results of a formation process. Therefore this formation process must provide the primary definition of sets and their properties. The categorial method is only an interesting secondary way of characterising these properties. Moreover some of the constructions of set theoretical entities in category theory are highly unnatural.

(2) Since some of the mappings (functors) of CS and topos theory can be defined in neither ZF nor NBG, these entities go beyond all the stages of the formation process for sets. How can there be any construction of mathematical objects beyond all the stages of set theory? And how can we avoid that these constructions lead to contradictions?

(3) How can set theory and category theory be unified? We have already seen that category theory contains entities which cannot be defined in set theory and class theory. Hence neither ZF nor NBG can be suitable frameworks for a unification. Therefore the established way to achieve a unification is topos theory. But as we saw, this leads directly to Problem (1). We still need a natural way to unify the two theories, which treats sets as sets and not only as objects in a category and which allows the smooth transition from set operations to category operations.

(III) My suggestion is that the switch from axiomatic set theory to operational set theory provides solutions to these three problems. First the set universe V is formed by iterating the set forming operations (real or imaginary) as far as possible. How can we make an imaginary jump out of V to the universe of CS or topos theory? We note that we have not made all imaginary jumps which are generally possible out of universes. We have done something more special. We have only made all possible imaginary jumps which are compatible with the preserved *transparency* of the classes. When we see a class from the inside, it is completely characterised by its members. After the jump out of the class/universe, when we see it as a set, the set is still completely characterised by its members. It remains transparent. Therefore it is logically possible that we make an imaginary jump out of the universe V of all sets if V by this operation loses its transparency. After the imaginary jump, V becomes a black box—just as in CS and topos theory. This solves Problem (2), and it also solves problems (1) and (3). By focusing on the operations, those which form the sets and those which lead to the universes of CS and topos theory, we get a natural, unified theory of sets and categories.

13 **Foundations of Mathematics**. (I) The two dominant proposals for a foundational system for classical mathematics are axiomatic set theory and topos theory. We have seen that none of them is adequate. Axiomatic set theory is incomplete as foundations because it does not allow the development of category theory within the set theoretical framework. Topos theory is in-

adequate because it conceptually presupposes set theory. My own proposal is that a mathematical theory of operations, including imaginary operations, should provide more adequate foundations of mathematics. Since every operation by Turing's thesis can be represented by a recursive function, the theory of computation in combination with logic is the proper foundations of mathematics. Another objection to axiomatic set theory and topos theory is that they cannot explain "the unreasonable effectiveness of mathematics" in physics. In contrast, a theory of operations can give such an explanation. The reason is that physics is concerned with such systems in the real world which can be defined by simple operational definitions. (It can even be argued that reality itself is operationally definable, as in Hansen (1996c).) By Turing's thesis, all such systems can be represented by recursive functions which are the entities studied in a mathematical theory of operations. (Incidentally, this also explains the "unreasonable" effectiveness of mathematics in logic because mathematical logic mostly studies recursively axiomatisable theories. For essentially the same reason, it also explains the "unreasonable" effectiveness of mathematics in computer science because computers are recursive systems and they do nothing but calculate recursive functions.)
(II) An important philosophy of mathematics is *structuralism*, the idea that:

(13-1) *Mathematics is the science of structure.*

In one version, due to the Bourbaki group, the structures are supplied by set theory. In a more recent version, due to Lawvere and Tierney, the structures come from category theory. Several objections can be raised against structuralism in mathematics, for instance:
(1) As we have seen, neither axiomatic set theory nor topos theory is adequate as foundations of mathematics. None of them supplies sufficiently much structure to suffice for all of mathematics. Considerations of structure no doubt play an immense role in mathematics; but they do so in connection with single problems and individual mathematical theories like real analysis, complex analysis, and geometries. The case for believing that there is one theory of mathematics that can supply all structures which are used or ever can be used in mathematics is weak.

(2) Logic is an integral part of every mathematical theory. The structural view on logic is adopted in formal logic. In Hansen (1996a), I showed that the formalisation of logic in an essential way distorts the logic.
(III) My own idea about the nature of mathematics is:

(13-2) *Mathematics is problem solving.*

The fundamental mathematical problems come from operationally definable reality. This philosophy avoids the problems hampering structuralism. Assuming that a human being is a Turing machine, every problem a human being can ask can be represented in a Turing machine and therefore in the mathematical theory of operations. The theory of Turing machines and recursive functions is the kernel of mathematics, but it is not the whole of mathematics. Gödel's incompleteness theorems show that the theory of operations cannot be the whole of mathematics. It must gradually be extended with the assumptions that are parts of those imaginary operations which are supplements to the concrete operations. This gives a third objection to structuralism in the philosophy of mathematics.
(3) Mathematics is problem solving. Then the concept of a problem is a fundamental concept in mathematics. In Section 1 of my essay "What the Liar Said to Grelling" in Johansson *et al.* (2009), I showed that this concept is open, that is, it has no well-defined class as its extension. There is no "the class of all problems." Consequently, no single axiomatic theory can supply all the structures about which it is possible to pose (mathematical) problems. On the other hand, mathematics based on operational foundations is itself open and can be arbitrarily extended to accommodate any upcoming mathematical problem.
14 **The ω-Rule.** We operate in the language L(PA) of Peano arithmetic PA. In this language, we can formulate the ω-*rule*. Let A(x) be a formula having only 'x' free. Then the ω-rule is the infinitary rule:

(14-1) From $|- A(0), |- A(1), \ldots$ infer $|- \forall x A(x)$

Let **N** be the standard model of PA, and let Th(**N**) be the set of all sentences of L(PA) which are true in **N**. Then Th(**N**) is complete arithmetic, and we have:

PA + the ω-rule = Th(**N**)

In (1996b), I prove a slightly stronger result: All arithmetical calculations plus the predicate logic for L(PA) plus the ω-rule yields complete arithmetic. Therefore all arithmetical theory is really implicit in the ω-rule together with the arithmetical calculations. Consensus among set theorists is that there is not and cannot be anything corresponding to the ω-rule for a set theory like ZF. I am not convinced about the correctness of this conclusion. If we compare the ω-rule with the induction principle, we see that while the induction principle is finitary, the ω-rule is essentially infinitary as can be inferred by Gödel's incompleteness theorem. In the sequence of applications of the ω-rule needed to obtain complete arithmetic, infinitely many involve a jump out of an infinite universe, just as in the set formation process. This gives a set theoretical interpretation of the ω-rule. My conjecture is that operational set theory amended with the ω-rule (set theoretically interpreted) implies solutions to problems which are unsolvable in ZFC. Possibly it might even hold and be provable that

ZF + the ω-rule = complete set theory

My hope is that the ω-rule for instance might help to solve the continuum problem in operational set theory.

15 Set Theoretical Existence. An axiomatic set theory like ZF contains a number of claims about the existence of sets. One axiom implies the existence of an empty set. The Power Set Axiom says that for every set X there is a set $P(X)$, called the power set of X, which contains all the subsets of X. A third axiom implies that there is an infinite set. It would seem that belief in ZF commits one to believe in the existence of the sets which can be proved in ZF to exist. Philosophically this is odd. Many, including myself, would be unwilling to admit the existence in the physical world of at least infinite sets and would also be unwilling to believe in a Platonic world inhabited by sets and other abstract entities.

Operational set theory solves this problem. Hereditarily finite sets can be constructed by recursive operations of a Turing machine. We may therefore either say that these sets do not exist in the physical world but can be constructed by recursive operations which do exist in the physical world or else say that these sets do exist because they can be identified with the systems of recursive operations by which they are constructed. From the point of view of operational set theory, the question of the existence of hereditarily finite sets is without real content. For infinite sets, the situation is different. As shown above, infinite sets are the results of one or more imaginary operations. Imaginary operations are hypothesised. Since they are the results of a hypothesis, they do not commit us to a belief in the existence of infinite sets—neither in the physical universe nor in a Platonic universe. Gödel has, in the incompleteness theorems, proved that such hypotheses on seeing a universe from the outside as an object can lead to powerful insights which cannot be attained without this kind of hypotheses. Such insights are the sole *raison d'être* of set theory.

16 REMARK. In the following paragraphs, I consider three different approaches to set theory: Zermelo's and Shoenfield's in ZFC, Klaus Grue's in Map theory; and I compare them with my own ideas about operational set theory outlined in the present essay. I make comments on the approaches, mostly from a philosophical point of view.

17 *ZFC*. ZFC is based on the cumulative type structure. It coincides with the universe of all sets. ZFC is an axiomatic theory. Some axioms express what sets exist in the universe. Thus the *Power Set Axiom* states that for any given set w there is a set, the power set $y = P(w)$, which contains all the subsets of w:

(17-1) $\forall w \, \exists y \, \forall x \, (x \in y \leftrightarrow \forall z \, (z \in x \rightarrow z \in w))$
The *Axiom of Infinity* asserts the existence of an infinite set:
(17-2) $\exists w \, (\emptyset \in w \wedge \forall x \, (x \in w \rightarrow$
$\exists z \, (z \in w \wedge \forall y \, (y \in z \leftrightarrow y \in x \vee y = x))))$
Other axioms express properties which all sets have. Thus the *Axiom of Extensionality* implies that every set is completely determined by its members:

(17-3) $\forall x \, \forall y \, (\forall z \, (z \in x \leftrightarrow z \in y) \rightarrow x = y)$

The justification given for the axioms is that they can be seen to be true in the cumulative type structure.

18 COMMENTS. (I) One very attractive feature of ZFC with the cumulative type structure is that it is quite a transparent theory. It is generally easy for a human mind to associate sets, properties, relations, functions, and facts in the cumulative type structure with expressions and sentences in the theory. Such transparency is essential when we do mathematics. In operational set theory an even greater transparency is achieved than in the cumulative type structure. Only greater transparency than in the cumulative type structure can lead to solutions to the problems which are unsolvable in ZFC.

(II) Now come some critical remarks on ZFC. ZFC contains axioms which state the existence of sets. For all we know, sets do not exist in the physical world. One reply to this objection is to claim that instead sets exist in a parallel world, a Platonic world. There is some indication that this was Zermelo's standpoint. But again, for all we know there is no Platonic world. Therefore reference to a Platonic world cannot be used to justify the axioms of set theory. Operational set theory, in contrast, is a conceptualistic theory. The meaning of set language and principles comes from the set forming operations of the mind, real or imaginary. One of the more amazing features of mathematics is its effectiveness in modelling physical systems. This feature will be inexplicable if the axioms of a foundational system like ZFC are justified with reference to a Platonic world rather than to the physical world to which mathematics is applied with such success. Finally, the fact that ZFC is an axiomatic system of what is the case in the universe of sets makes it impossible to unify set theory and category theory. In operational set theory, a simple and natural unification is achieved.

(III) Shoenfield's way of developing the cumulative type structure is not Platonist. Therefore Shoenfield does not justify the axioms of ZFC with reference to a Platonic world. For Shoenfield, the cumulative type structure is a fiction arising as the result of a mental process. This is progress compared to the Platonist approach. The quotation in § 6 shows the beginning of an operational analysis of sets. A comparison with Analysis 7 shows, however, that Shoenfield's analysis is somewhat superficial. Important components in an adequate investigation of operationally defined sets are missing. The other two objections to the Platonist approach to set theory above apply even to Shoenfield's version of operational set theory. He has no explanation of why the operations used to build sets are important. In particular, he cannot explain the effectiveness of set theory in modelling physical systems. Since Shoenfield stays with the axiomatic approach, he leaves no room for a unification of set theory and category theory.

19 **Map Theory**. The Danish mathematician and computer scientist Klaus Grue has developed a set theory called *map theory (MT)* which in its methodology is very different from ZFC. (See Grue (1992, 2002, 2007) and Berline and Grue (1997).) Grue (2007) writes: "MT is slightly more powerful than ZFC set theory, but its merit is that it builds on top of computable functions where ZFC builds on top of finite sets. Thus, where ZFC is suited as a foundation of mathematics, MT is suited as a foundation of both mathematics and computer science."

I now give a compact summary of the main tenets of MT. It takes as its starting point the traditional λ–calculus. The original form of Church's thesis is:

Let $f: \underline{N}^n \to \underline{N}$. Then f is computable iff f is definable in the λ–calculus.

Thus from the outset, all computable (recursive) functions are present in MT. The strategy in MT is to show how computable functions can be used to generate a theory of hereditarily finite sets and then generalise this approach to infinite sets. Let r and s be two closed terms, i.e., terms without free variables. r and s are equivalent, r ≡ s, if they compute all closed terms t as input with the same result. A *map* is a ≡-equivalence class. From this definition, we eventually get immediately the axiom of extensionality of ZFC. The axioms of MT fall naturally in four groups depending on what they concern: λ-calculus, sentential logic, first-order predicate logic, set theory. To redo ZFC in MT, we must define classical first-order logic in MT. Since truth functions are recursive, sentential logic is easily introduced. To introduce the universal and existential operators and set theory into MT, we have to leave the realm of computable functions. The language of MT is expanded with Hilbert's ε–operator. If A = A(x) is a formula in a predicate logical language, then εx A(x) is a term which denotes an arbitrary individual which satisfies A(x) if there is such an object. Thus ε is a choice operator. The quantifiers can then be defined as follows:

$$\exists x\, A(x) \leftrightarrow A(\varepsilon x\, A(x))$$
$$\forall x\, A(x) \leftrightarrow \neg\exists x\neg A(x) \leftrightarrow \neg\neg A(\varepsilon x\, (\neg A)) \leftrightarrow A(\varepsilon x\, (\neg A))$$

These ideas can be implemented in MT. Given the ε-operator, it is easy to derive the axiom of choice in MT. The last group of axioms certify that we get the right subclass of the class of maps as representatives of sets and that the sets have the properties attributed to sets in ZFC, including well-foundedness. Maps which are well-founded are called *classical maps*. The subdomain *C* consisting of the class of classical maps contains the sets of MT. There is no axiom in MT which directly represents the axiom of infinity in ZF; but it can be proven that the image of *C* under a classical map is small enough to be considered a set rather than a proper class and that the image under some classical maps is large enough to be considered infinite.

20 COMMENTS. (I) Map theory is a remarkable and ingenious construction. It is of considerable logical and mathematical interest in its own right; but it is unclear whether it really has capability to generate any essential new insights into the nature of sets. Only a careful analysis can decide that, and such an analysis is by no means trivial because of the complexity and opaqueness of MT.

(II) Map theory is worked out on top of the λ-calculus. The λ-calculus is a calculus for functional expressions. Arguably it gives the most general notation for the definition of computable functions. Therefore λ-calculus, and hence also map theory, changes the focus from the meaning of functional expressions to the functional expressions themselves. Because of this, map theory can maybe be characterised as a nominalistic theory of sets. I have, for instance in Hansen (2007), argued that properties, relations, functions—and hence also their extensions, sets—can only be understood conceptualistically. Operational set theory is clearly a theory which is conceptualistic in character.

(III) The lambda-calculus is an opaque theory. Map theory is even more so. In contrast, ZFC is a transparent theory of sets. It is easy to see immediately what sets, operations and facts, the terms and statements in ZFC refer to. In operational set theory, an even greater transparency is achieved. Those problems which are unsolvable in ZFC demand for their solution more transparency than is present in ZFC with the cumulative type structure, not less.

It is to the credit of operational set theory that it implies a simple and natural solution to one such problem, the problem of unifying set theory and category theory. Though the details of the unification are not worked out in the present article, it is fairly easy to see that it can be done. Such unification cannot be achieved in ZFC, and MT has nothing to contribute to a solution either. This shows that MT is only to a limited extent an operational set theory. Essentially it succeeds only as an operational set theory for hereditarily finite sets. There is no understanding in MT of the imaginary operations which are essential in infinite sets and important parts of the analysis of infinite sets in operational set theory.

(IV) A set theory involving infinite sets cannot be computable. Mathematicians can handle infinities only by conceptualisation and not by calculation. Grue proudly declares: "Thus, where ZFC is suited as a foundation of mathematics, MT is suited as a foundation of both mathematics and computer science." But is it really of any value to try to find common foundations of mathematics and computer science? Sufficiently efficient machine calculations are the business of computer science. Though calculations are at the bottom of all mathematics, mathematicians solve problems which go beyond what is computable and can only be handled by conceptualisation and insights into concepts and operations, both real and imaginary. Mathematics and computer science have less in common than a first impression might indicate.

21 NOTE. The present paper contains the basic ideas in a research program for set theory. As such it is necessarily sketchy. I have tried to expose the conceptual and ontological ideas in this program in as simple and intuitive a way as I can and I hope that at least a few readers will be able to see the vision behind the program as clearly as I feel I do. The ideas in Analysis 7 on operational set theory, based on real and imaginary operations, are original. The seven suggestions on applications of operational set theory in §§ 9–15 are also original.

References

Berline, C., and K. Grue (1997). "A κ-denotational Semantics for Map Theory in ZFC+SI." *Theoretical Computer Science* 179, no. 1–2: 137–202.

Drake, F. (1974). *Set Theory: An Introduction to Large Cardinals*. North-Holland Publishing Company, Amsterdam.

Grue, K. (1992). "Map Theory." *Theoretical Computer Science* 102, no. 1: 1–133.

Grue, K. (2002). "Lambda-Calculus as a Foundation for Mathematics." In C. A. Anderson and M. Zeleny, editors, *Logic, Meaning, and Computation: Essays in Memory of Alonzo Church*, Kluwer, Dordrecht.

Grue, K. (2007). "A Gentle Introduction to Map Theory." Accessible on Klaus Grue's homepage.

Hansen, K. B. (1996a). *Applied Logic*. Chapter 2, "Conditionals and the Foundations of Logic." Acta Universitatis Upsaliensis, Uppsala.

Hansen, K. B. (1996b). *Applied Logic*. Chapter 7, "Questions and Results on ω-Consistency." Acta Universitatis Upsaliensis, Uppsala.

Hansen, K. B. (1996c). *Logical Physics: Quantum Reality Theory.* Library of Theoria, Thales, Stockholm.

Hansen, K. B. (2007). "Remarks on Wittgenstein's Philosophy: Private Language and Meaning." *Danish Yearbook of Philosophy* 42: 33–73.

Hatcher, W. S. (1982). *The Logical Foundations of Mathematics*. Pergamon Press, Oxford.

Johansson, L.-G., E. Carlson and R. Sliwinski (eds.) (2009), Logic, Ethics, and All That Jazz. Uppsala Philosophical Studies, Uppsala.

Shoenfield, J. R. (1967). *Mathematical Logic*. Addison-Wesley, Reading MA.

Shoenfield, J. R. (1977). "Axioms of Set Theory." In J. Barwise (ed.), *Handbook of Mathematical Logic*. North-Holland Publishing Company, Amsterdam.

Smorynski, C. (1977). "The Incompleteness Theorems." In J. Barwise (ed.), *Handbook of Mathematical Logic*. North-Holland Publishing Company, Amsterdam.

KNOWING ONESELF?
AN ESSAY ON COMTEAN SKEPTICISM ABOUT
INTROSPECTIVE SELF-OBSERVATION[1]

CHRISTIAN BEENFELDT

University of Copenhagen

"With little examination," Russell Hurlburt and Eric Schwitzgebel have observed, "introspection has re-entered psychology and philosophy. Even hard-nosed cognitive neuroscientists ask their subjects about their subjectively felt experience while in the fMRI magnet" (Hurlburt and Schwitzgebel 2007, 5).

William James—at least at the time when he wrote *The Principles of Psychology*—might well have approved of this development. Introspective observation, as he put it, "is what we have to rely on first and foremost and always" (James 1952, 121, italics removed). When we introspect we look into our own minds and report what we find there, namely states of consciousness. This James takes to be an established fact, accepted by all sides in the debate at the time. As he put it, "[e]very one agrees that we there discover states of consciousness. So far as I know, the existence of such states has never been doubted by any critic, however skeptical in other respects he may have been" (James 1952, 121, italics removed). Indeed, "[a]ll people unhesitatingly believe that they feel themselves thinking, and that they distinguish the mental state as an inward activity or passion, from all the objects with which it may cognitively deal. I regard this belief as the most fundamental of all the postulates of Psychology" (James 1952, 121).[2]

James contracted to write his great textbook of psychology in 1880 and a decade later the monumental work was finished. According to the eminent Harvard historian of psychology, Edwin Boring, the pro-introspection attitude expressed by James was shared by the philosophers, physiologists, and physicists who founded modern scientific psychology in the 1850s, 1860s and 1870s, including "Fechner, Lotze, Helmholtz, Wundt, Hering, Mach and their associates" (Boring 1953, 171). It seems clear that James and the other founders of psychology who shared his belief in the fundamental role of introspection in psychology—as well as contemporary psychologists, philosophers, and neuroscientists who have invited introspection back into their respective fields—all share a certain basic philosophical supposition (tacitly held, perhaps). The supposition is that introspection is a *possible* act to perform.

Comte's Denial of Introspection

Auguste Comte famously denied this supposition. According to him, the very notion of introspection, of interior observation ("l'observation intérieure"), is a "fundamental sophism" and "pure illusion" (Comte 1988, 20). It amounts to the "the supposition of a man seeing himself think"—a clear "absurdity" (Comte 1855, 383). Comte's denial of introspection was formulated when scientific psychology was in its infancy, exercising a clear influence upon both its formative and subsequent development (Hatfield 2005, 271–72).

We will consider some of Comte's objections to introspection in this paper.[3] The aim will be to take the Comtean criticism of introspection as the point of embarkation for an exploration of some general philosophical considerations regarding introspective self-observation. This paper is *not* intended as a contribution to systematic and scholarly Comte history, nor as an excursion into critical exegesis. No general assessment or evaluation of Comte's overall philosophy will be put forward. We will consider only Comte's arguments *against* introspection, as these are made in his *Course on Positive Philosophy*[4]—a work otherwise dominated by the ambitions of furnishing a comprehensive, systematic, and constructive methodological project (Gane 2006, 2–6). Only Comte's famous objections to introspection, as these have been generally received, will be our concern.

We begin by making a few prefatory remarks about Comte and his times. Born on January 19 in 1798, in Montpellier near the Southern coast of France, Comte came to the world as the French Revolution was ending, he was a young child when Napoleon Bonaparte declared himself emperor, and he was a teenager when the Battle of Waterloo was fought. In this atmosphere of social havoc and unrestrained radical thought, he developed a system of philosophy—*positivism*—envisioned as a comprehensive, secularized religion of science and humanity.

In the post-Napoleonic age, Comte's positivism was a significant intellectual force. According to John Stuart Mill, this view, "to which the name of M. Comte is more identified than any other" (Mill 1961, 3), was the subject of much discussion in mid-nineteenth century intellectual circles—in both England and on the Continent (Mill 1961, 1).[5] As Comte saw it, he had in the system of positivism identified "a great fundamental law, to which the mind is subjected by an invariable necessity." This law states that each branch of human knowledge "passes in succession through three different theoretical states"—the (1) theological, (2) metaphysical, and (3) scientific or positive state (Comte 1988, 1–2)—in a trajectory of societal evolution passing from the most primitive to the most enlightened.

> Far from a proponent of pure, objective, socially neutral science, Comte launched the discipline he named "sociology" as an inquiry into a given stage of civilization's state of knowledge and key functions. (Tresch 2011, 672)

As far as the study of human mental life is concerned, it is at the positive state to be dispensed with entirely, in favor of the new discipline of *social physics* (Comte 1988, 13). Psychology, as a posited field of enquiry, was thus viewed by Comte with clear disapproval. In "no case is there room for *that illusory psychology*—the last transformation of theology—the revival of which attempts are being made so vainly at the present day" (Comte 1988, 20; italics added). Much hinges on defeating such vain attempts. Psychology, as Comte saw it, stands in the way of achieving the enlightened stage of development throughout the full domain of human knowledge, when "the philosophical system of the modern world will be founded at last in its entirety" (Comte 1988, 13).

If psychology is a dead weight restraining our ascension to the supreme stage of development, the supposed mental activity of introspection amounts to the solid lead core of that encumbrance. This is due to the *spuriously observational nature of introspection*. Indeed, the only hope the proponents of psychology have to "check the decadence of their pretended science, is by showing that their doctrines are "founded upon the observation of facts" (Comte 1988, 20). Attempting to do so, they have "by a very singular subtlety," posited two "kinds of observation of equal importance, the one exterior, the other interior, the latter being devoted solely to the study of intellectual phenomena" (Comte 1988, 20). This supposed interior observation, however, is a counterfeit posit. It is an impossible act to perform, because

> in the case of intellectual phenomena, to observe them in this manner while they are taking place is clearly out of the question. The thinking individual cannot cut himself in two—one of the parts reasoning, while the other is looking on. Since in this case the organ observed and the observing organ are identical, how could any observation be made? The principle of this so-called psychological method is therefore entirely worthless. (Comte 1988, 21)

To begin, let us fix our attention on the following part of this pregnant statement: "Since in this case the organ observed and the observing organ are identical, how could any observation be made?" (Comte 1988, 21). On a simple and straightforward reading, the argument seems to be that introspection, understood at the neuroanatomic and neurophysiological level, involves the organ of the brain[6] observing itself. This activity, however, is not possible for that organ to carry out. By way of analogy, think of the absurdity involved in seeking to use an ordinary kitchen knife to cut itself in half. If we give the matter some thought, however, it seems clear that this line of reasoning carries little power to convince. It is impossible for an ordinary kitchen knife to cut itself in half. But is it really impossible for an organ to observe itself? There seems to be no ineludible biological or metaphysical reason why this would be so. Comte, it fact, was here relying on a phrenological understanding of neuroanatomy.

Phrenology, a widespread and popular view of brain, mind, and character in the nineteenth century, largely developed out of the "Schädellehre" (doctrine of the skull) of Franz-Joseph Gall (1758–1828). According to the principles of phrenology, (1) the brain is the organ of the mind, (2) each mental power or faculty is robustly localized in a specific region of the brain, (3) the relative size of each respective region is a measure of articulation in a given individual of the corresponding mental faculty, and (4) the surface structure of the skull faithfully reflects the topography of the brain.[7] Points (3) and (4), in particular, gave rise to the famous phrenological method known as "cranioscopy," i.e. the pseudoscientific procedure of examining the surface features of the skull as means of obtaining knowledge about the individual's personality, intellect, and moral character.[8]

We will here focus our attention on points (1) and (2). Doing so, we can put the Comtean criticism of introspection as follows: Just as a kitchen knife can only cut objects that are spatially distinct from itself (e.g. a tomato on the kitchen table), not itself—so the region of the brain dedicated to observation can only observe or introspect *other* regions of the brain, not itself. We see this sort of reasoning at work when Comte grants that it *is* possible, to some extent at least, to introspect the goings-on in the *spatially distinct* brain regions dedicated to the passions. As he put it, such self-observation of the passions is possible "for the *anatomical reason* that the organs which are [the seat of the passions] are distinct from those whose function are devoted to observation" (Comte 1988, 21, italics added). (Comte was speaking of the localized regions of the brain as individual "organs.")

Despite the strongly voiced conclusion of his anti-introspective statement in the *Cours*, Comte's anatomical line of reasoning regarding the impossibility of introspection is quite unconvincing. While there clearly is some localization of function in the brain, phrenological theory is now viewed on all sides as a complete mistake. The brain is not a collection of nation-state-like sovereign domains, each dedicated to different mental faculties and partitioned by means of inflexible and impenetrable borders.

Yet, Comte's argument about self-observing organs can still serve as a stimulus to philosophical thought regarding the nature of organs and self-observation. Setting aside the notion of a localized part of the brain being the "observing organ," we might more plausibly consider the *brain as a whole* to be the relevant cellular segment capable of making observation. Can this organ observe itself? From a biological perspective, a strong case can be made to the effect that the brain has been evolutionarily shaped and molded as an *outwards-directed* organ—an organ that relies on world-directed sensory receptors (eyes, ears and so on) to register and interact with objects in the external world (predators, prey, food and mates). If we focus only on patent adaptive benefits, the brain, the nervous system, and the sensory organs, all clearly serve vital outward-directed functions.

This reasoning, however, falls short of showing any metaphysical limitation on the nature of observing organs per se. Philosophically, in other words, the adaptive evolutionary function of our highly evolved brain carries little significance vis-à-vis the metaphysical possibility of introspection. Unlike the physical impossibility of an ordinary kitchen knife cutting itself in half, a "brain" *is* able to observe itself in rather straightforward ways. A man can observe himself merely by looking in a mirror. The man's brain, in an odd manner of speaking, is thus observing itself. If one thinks that the skull stands in the way of such an observation, we might imagine that this bony structure has been peeled off in preparation for drastic neurosurgery, and that the patient is inspecting his own organ of awareness in an overhead mirror. Tactile perception is a form of sensory observation, so if one thinks that specular reflection of light afforded by the polished mirror surfaces does not qualify as *direct* observation, we might imagine (somewhat disturbingly) that that the patient palpates his own brain and, thereby, directly observes his own organ of observation. To return to visual perception, a de-skulled creature with an abnormally extended optic nerve, ophthalmic artery and so on, could directly see itself by lifting up the eye and pointing it downwards.[9]

To defend the claim that organs, and specifically brains—again, in a very odd manner of speaking—can observe themselves, one must not (and one certainly should not), assume that they are capable of doing so *in vacuo*. In all of these examples, the brain isn't doing *anything* as an isolated organ. To see, one must both have a brain, an eye, a respiratory system etc. A functioning, conscious brain must be continuously nourished and maintained. It is a segment of a living organism that continuously interacts with the surrounding world. A brain, no more than an arm or a lung, can exist and function in isolation.[10] In Bennett and Hacker's formulation, the "organs of an animal are part of the animal, and psychological predicates are ascribable to the whole animal, not to its constituent parts" (Bennett and Hacker 2004, 73)—in other words, observation is an activity performed only by the whole living organism, not by any constituent cellular segment.

The Inner Eye

Setting aside the issue of brains and self-observing organs, let us consider the question of introspection from the *mental* side. Let us begin by considering the sentence from Comte immediately preceding the one about self-observing organs: "The thinking individual cannot cut himself in two—one of the parts reasoning, while the other is looking on" (Comte 1988, 21). Is *this* a good argument against introspection? It may be—*if* one holds a certain distinctive view of introspection and, more broadly, of mind and body. The view I have in mind was described by Charles Siewert as involving either the claim

> that consciousness is in some sense the "perception" of mental items of some sort, or else the claim that some general analogy between consciousness and sense-perception provides us with an account of what is special about the former. (Siewert 1998, 16)

Siewert speaks of this conception of introspection as one of the major strands making up the "Cartesian View" of psychological knowledge. Preceding (and influencing)[11] Descartes' views of psychology, this conception of introspection as an "inner sense"[12] or the "mind's eye" can be traced back to Saint Augustine (354–430).

In the *Confessions*, Augustine describes remembrance as entering "a great field or a spacious palace, a storehouse for countless images of all kinds which are conveyed to it by the senses" (Augustine 1986, 214). Inside this immense inner storehouse he finds a retained mental copy of the things sensed, enabling him to inspect them again whenever he wishes. "In it are the sky, the earth, and the sea, ready at my summons, together with everything that I have ever perceived in them by my senses, except the things which I have forgotten". (Augustine 1986, 215)

> [M]en go out and gaze in astonishment at high mountains, the huge waves off the sea, the broad reaches of rivers, the ocean that encircles the world, or the stars in their courses. But they pay no attention to themselves. They do not marvel at the thought that while I have been mentioning these things, I have not been looking at them with my eyes, and that I could not even speak of mountains or waves, rivers or stars, which are things I have seen, or of the ocean, which I know only on the evidence of others, unless I could see them *in my mind's eye*, in my memory, and with the same vast space between them that would be there if I were looking at them in the world outside myself… They are not inside me themselves, but only their images. (Augustine 1986, 216; italics added)

According to William Lyons, "Augustine [suggested] something that became the orthodox view from roughly the end of the Middle Ages to the beginning of our century," namely that we can discover the nature of mind by "engaging directly or indirectly in some process of inner perception or inner observation" (Lyons 1986, 2).

Taking this notion of the inner eye in a rather literal sense, the problem is apparent. How can this eye see itself? Normal eyes, after all, see everything *except* themselves. And mental eyes (*res cogitans*, as it were, not *res extensa*) presumably have no mirror reflection. Yet even against this view, the anti-introspection argument seems fairly weak. A Cartesian could grant that the inner eye, unable to see *itself*, can still can see *everything else*—all the images of memory and imagination, and the whole mental world. Perhaps it is impossible to introspect one's own organ of introspection, just as it would be impossible to see one's own eyes in a world with no reflecting surfaces. But this makes introspection no less possible than perceptual awareness of one's environment would be in a completely mirrorless world.

Is this a line of argument a strict Cartesian could accept? Perhaps not. After all, if one presses home the analogy between the mind's eye and a normal eye, one also presses home the implied separation between the internal seeing-eye and the internal object-seen. This makes it difficult to maintain that the mind is an indivisible Cartesian substance. Recall Comte's argument that the "thinking individual cannot cut himself in two" (Comte 1988, 21). As Fred Wilson argued in the paper, "Mill and Comte on the Method of Introspection," Comte is here calling attention to the profound challenges that mind, understood as an indivisible, simple substance capable of becoming aware of itself, poses for Cartesian philosophy:

> How can the mind become aware of itself? That would require that it become a property of itself. But that is impossible: substances are not properties. Or if it can somehow become a property of itself, then it becomes independent of itself, as any substance is independent of its properties. In that case, however, the part can cease to be present to the consciousness, and the mind ceases to be a simple substance. Descartes wrestled with these problems.... (Wilson 1991, 115)

Wilson concludes that "Comte's point is a strong one"—strong, that is, if one accepts the Cartesian substance view of the mind.

For the purpose of the present discussion, we are happy to let Wilson's defense of Comte's argument against the possibility of introspection stand uncontested. It is quite plausible that Comte's argument offers a good reason *not* to be a Cartesian dualist. But there are already many, *many* other good reasons not to be a Cartesian dualist. The mind is no Cartesian substance. It is a basic biological capacity of certain highly evolved organisms that have sufficiently sophisticated cyto-structures of neurons and supporting cells. It is a natural, organic, biological capacity, capable of development, injury, and degeneration—not a celestial Cogito.

Setting aside the Cartesian notion of an indivisible mind, however, can Comte's argument be brought to bear upon more plausible theories of mind and introspection? Yes, arguably so, if one understands Comte's critique of the divided mind—of the thinking individual cutting himself in two—in a *temporal* rather than a spatial sense. This version of the argument, then, calls attention to the evident temporal requirement of introspection. As Comte argued,

> [i]n order to observe, *your intellect must pause from activity*; yet it is this very activity that you want to observe. If you can not effect the pause, you can not observe: *if you do effect it, there is nothing to observe.* (Comte 1855, 33, italics added)

There are really two claims here, namely (1) that in order to be introspectively aware of current conscious activity, you must pause that activity (e.g. you must stop solving the mathematical problem to be aware that you are, in fact, engaging in quantitative thinking) and (2) that by pausing of the current cognitive activity you wipe the cognitive slate clean as it were, leaving "nothing to observe." Since it may well be the case, at least in certain circumstances, that a pause (or even just a split-second delay as one switches attention) is inherent in the act of introspectively observing and identifying mental content, we will allow that (1) has some plausibility. The error lies in (2), the supposition that any mental switch, shift, break or pause in attention, however brief, erases, removes or makes inaccessible the previous mental activity and content.[13]

John Stuart Mill made this point rather well. In *Auguste Comte and Positivism*,[14] Mill generously praises Comte's overall project,[15] but he also voices strong disagreement with Comte's rejection of introspection.[16] This view represents, he complains, a "grave aberration in M. Comte's view of the method of positive science" (Mill 1961, 62–63). To meet this aberration, Mill offers two devastating answers to Comte's arguments against introspection. First, Mill points out that there is such a phenomenon as *divided attention*. We are able to pay attention to more than thing at the same time. "It is true that attention may be weakened by being divided" but, as he puts it, "a difficulty is not an impossibility" (Mill 1961, 64). Second, Mill points out that we have the faculty of *memory*. "[A] fact may be studied through the medium of memory, not at the very moment of our perceiving it, but the moment after; and this is really the mode in which our best knowledge of our intellectual states is generally acquired" (Mill 1961, 64).

Mill was right. While our attentive resources are highly circumscribed, we *can* pay attention to more than one thing at the same time. Of course, much hinges on precisely what attentive regard is taken to mean. If it means what cognitive psychologists today call *working memory capacity*, we have an attentive power of perhaps five to nine items, as George Miller famously showed (Miller 1956). Subsequent researchers have argued for a slightly lower number of items or "chunks" of information, perhaps on the order of four (Cowan 2001). Mill himself cited contemporary work in psychology (by Sir William Hamilton) that showed an attentive power of as many as six items, but added, wisely, that it "is probable that different minds have the power in different degrees" (Mill 1961, footnote 64). Further, we clearly do *retain* experience on a moment-to-moment basis. The sharp pain delivered by a dentist's drill is not erased from our recollection the very moment that the rotating metal no longer touches our exposed root canal. Nor, indeed, does the delayed application of anesthesia to the region *immediately* remove our remembrance of the pain. Having made the rebuttal of Comte's temporal argument, Mill leaves the topic and moves on to discuss and assess Comte's theory of society. Is seems, though, that we might profitably expand Mill's line of argument quite a bit further, and apply it to cognitive activity in general.

To state the point compactly, we should recognize that information retention is a basic and ineliminable feature of our cognitive capacities in general. In the most basic case, consider the role played by our ability to carry information when we simply *perceive* our environment. In visual perception, we do not absorb all the visual features in a flash, like an old-fashioned camera where the emulsion of light-sensitive silver halide salts on the film surface form an image in response to optical lens-focused electromagnetic radiation (and suitable post-exposure chemical processing). Rather, our eyes dart about in constant, high-speed saccadic motion, taking in selected parts of the complex scenery. The brain retains the acquired information and we cognize the scene as a whole, not as a fragmented string of momentary flashes. We do not "see" the saccades, of course, but we may notice moving our head around, tilting it up and down, left and right, as we take in the surroundings. Across each moment-to-moment interval, information is retained. The same is true of auditory perception. Without the ability to retain auditory information from moment to moment, we could not compare two tones, let alone hear a melody. Nor could we have a conversation. Or even walk down the street to buy groceries.

Put provocatively, the vast balance of our perceptual awareness is actually "retro-perceptive"—it is *retained* information, ultimately originating in the complex stimulation of sensory receptors and the transduction of energy through the relevant neural pathways; it is not a staccato-like state that turns on and off in synchronicity with momentary cellular stimulation. Like perception, more sophisticated acts of cognition also depend, crucially, on our ability to carry information from one moment to the next. Thinking, for example, draws on the abundant store of semantic memory that we have acquired and retained across a lifetime. On the level of self-directed rather than subpersonal activity, a process of thinking requires one to keep overall context and purpose in mind across a span of time, to remember key assumptions, evidence, intermediate conclusions and so on. If attention wanders, the cognitive slate is not erased. One, rather (in most cases anyway) retains the information and returns to the cognitive task at hand. Reading, to take a different example, "does not occur in a moment" either, as Neisser observed many years ago. During reading the "information on the printed page becomes available to the reader only over time, and reading must be organized over time as well" (Neisser 1976, 14). Not just reading "but also listening, feeling, and looking are skillful activities that occur over time" (Neisser 1976, 14).

Introspective awareness is no different than perception, thinking or reading in this respect—it too requires the retention of information across time. What one just did, or thought, or felt, or experienced, is not a momentary point, with no extension and no temporal duration. I recall, for example, thinking about a certain mathematical proof even as I stop for a moment and wonder whether I have been spending too much time doing math and too little time listening to Beethoven. Put more polemically, if one thinks reliance on retained information invalidates a cognitive capacity, one is advancing skepticism of a very radical sort. Even the mighty daemon from the *Meditations* allowed Descartes his Cogito. "Sum," after all, requires the moment-to-moment retention of "Cogito" and "Ergo," to become a meaningful cognitive whole.

It might, of course, be argued that the "Cogito," as Descartes conceives of it, is an *instantaneous insight*, not a temporal one. Descartes' own formulations, however, speaks against this interpretation. When he introduces the "Cogito" early in the *Meditations*, he treats both the (clearly temporal) physical utterance of the "Cogito" and the mental conception of it, as comparable:

> Thus, after everything has been most carefully weighed, it must finally be established that this pronouncement 'I am, I exist' is necessarily true every time I utter it or conceive it in my mind. (Descartes 1993, 64, italics added)

Further, the temporal identity of the "Cogito" is assumed when he ponders the following problem:

> I am; I exist—this is certain. But for how long? For as long as I am thinking; for perhaps it could also come to pass that if I were to cease all thinking I would then utterly cease to exist. (Descartes 1993, 65)

Nothing much hinges on this point. Regardless of how Descartes may have conceived of the "Cogito," we should certainly grant that all thought takes time, however little. If so, some temporal retention—even on the scale of milliseconds—must be assumed. Apart from this point, the further philosophical intricacies of temporal consciousness will not be broached here. The point is one cannot point disparagingly to the moment-to-moment retention requirements of introspection alone. *This feature* is shared by all cognitive processes alike. A skeptic who denies the possibility of introspection because it inherently involves moment-to-moment information retention, must also deny the possibility of all our other mental capacities—for they too, in the same manner, necessarily requiring retained information across a span of time.

Ryle's "Comtean" Argument

Consider, now, a version of the Comtean case against introspection that, rather than making a global claim regarding the nature of the mental, focuses on *selected individual states* to its point. Gilbert Ryle advances an argument of this sort in *The Concept of Mind* (Ryle traces it back, incidentally, to Hume and not to Comte). Ryle contends that "[n]o one could introspectively scrutinize the state of panic or fury, since the dispassionateness exercised in scientific observation is, by the definition of 'panic' and 'fury', not the state of mind of the victim of those turbulences" (Ryle 2000, 159). This applies, Ryle maintains, more broadly than simply to the passions. "[S]ince a convulsion of merriment is not the state of mind of the sober experimentalist," as he puts it, "the enjoyment of a joke is also not an introspectible happening" (Ryle 2000, 159). Accordingly, "[s]tates of mind such as these more or less violent agitations can be examined only in retrospect" (Ryle 2000, 159).[17]

Are there, as Ryle maintains, states where introspective *scrutiny*—requiring "the dispassionateness exercised in scientific observation"—is rendered impossible? Surely, something *defined* from the very outset as requiring "dispassionateness" cannot be exercised by an individual exhibiting great passionateness, as it were. So the answer, trivially, is affirmative. But much, here, seems to ride on Ryle's choice of polar opposites: on the one hand, we have the act of calmly identifying one's current mental goings-on, understood as the attempt to "introspectively *scrutinize*" one's own mind—and, on the other hand, we have extreme emotive responses such as panic, fury and not just merriment, but "*convulsion* of merriment." "East is East, and West is West" as Kipling said, "and never the twain shall meet."

When might one feel panic? Consider the following example. You are driving on the freeway and a few hundred yards ahead you suddenly see a wrong-way driver heading straight towards you. Presumably the demand characteristics of the situation as well as the intensity of the emotional responses one would experience, so completely absorbs one's attentive capacity that one is incapable of pausing and engaging in introspective scrutiny. "When the truck came towards us, I just pressed the brake pedal as hard as I could and I kept pressing it, and kept pressing it, till long after the car had stopped. I don't know what I was thinking. I guess I must have panicked."

We have all heard (on television, if not in real life) victims of extreme circumstances recount their experiences in such dramatic words. It seems rather plausible that, in such cases, the capacity for sophisticated cognition and refined self-reflection all but shuts down. It is, similarly, difficult to imagine someone being able to complete a complex mathematical proof in a situation like this. It makes good evolutionary sense, then, that the demand characteristics of life-threatening circumstances all but preclude the exercise of certain kinds of absorbing, volitional cognitive processes. Introspection is, on most accounts anyway, a fairly sophisticated cognitive process. Exercising it requires, if nothing else, an expenditure of nontrivial attentional resources. Yet, emotional responses such as panic and fury, by their nature, arise in dramatic ("attention-grabbing") situations where we pay maximal attention to external reality, and not to our own mental goings-on—and where we would find it very difficult, if not impossible, to maintain a sustained process of introspective reflection.

We, and indeed all mammals, have a visual blind spot—a scotoma in the field of vision caused by the absence of photoreceptors at the point where the retinal ganglion cell axons of the optic nerve exit the retina. We respond with audition to only a range of possible cycle-per-second frequency vibrations, usually from 20Hz to 20,000Hz. Outside this range we do not hear the stimulus. Memory is limited by factors such as exposure time, frequency, fact type, fact salience, event violence, stress, expectations and so on.[18] Similar limitations are found with respect to all our sensory and cognitive capacities. There are, surely, also limitations on our ability to exercise self-directed attention and reflection. The fact that we are not be able to engage in certain kinds of introspective self-reflection under certain exigent circumstances, may well be one such limitation. But this constitutes no more epistemic grounds for skeptically rejecting introspection than, say, the limitations on the response-range of our chemoreceptors constitute epistemic grounds for dismissing olfaction.

Comte Misunderstood?

In the paper "Mill's Misreading of Comte on 'Interior Observation'" published by the *Journal of the History of Philosophy*, Scharff argues that Comte's critique of introspection has been misunderstood by Mill and by subsequent thinkers alike.

> Comte's critique is … entirely retrospective and anti-metaphysical. For him, *l'observation intérieure* is a specious operation modeled

after Descartes's meditation: it is practiced by incurably prescientific thinkers like Cousin and Jouffroy; and it leads to speculative doctrines about the Mind, or Self, as such. (Scharff 1989, 571)

Scharff puts forward this claim again in the 2002 book, *Comte after Positivism*, arguing that Mill misunderstood "Comte's villain," "l'observation intérieure" (Scharff 2002, 19).

Scharff, however, *also* grants that "Comte inserts no science between biology and sociology" (Scharff 1989, 571)—i.e. he recognizes that Comte allowed no legitimate place in the order of knowledge for scientific psychology as such. This clearly points to a far more wide-reaching anti-psychological stance on Comte's part, than a mere denial of incurably prescientific Cartesianism would lead one to expect. This observation, incidentally, is entirely in line with Mill's reading of the *Cours:*

> [Comte] rejects totally, as an invalid process, psychological observation properly so called, or in other words, internal consciousness, at least as regards our intellectual operations. He gives no place in his series to the science of Psychology, and always speaks of it with contempt. The study of mental phenomena, as he expresses it ... [is in his scheme] a branch of physiology. (Mill 1961, 62)

As Mazlish sums up the Comte-Mill disagreement:

> Fundamental to Mill's differences with Comte was their opposed positions on psychology. Comte ... refused to recognize the existence of a possible positive subject. After biology there was sociology; psychological phenomena simply disappear or were resolved into biology or sociology. In fact, when pressed by Mill, Comte suggested that phrenology was the true science—a physiological one—which explained all of the phenomena supposedly imputed to a so-called psychological domain.... (Mazlish 1975, 260)[19]

To carry the weight of such an assignment, Comte *should have* denied our ability to know our own minds by direct self-observation.[20] If Comte meant only to deny Cartesianism, we have no quibble with the target—only with the implication that the essential Cartesian error was the notion of *retained cognitive content across time*. Moment-to-moment information retention across time is the *sin qua non*—not just of introspection, but of our psychological capabilities in general. If Comte meant to reject not just Cartesian introspection, but introspection more broadly and more plausibly conceived, we follow Mill in rejecting his rejection.

Notes

1 Research for this paper was supported by a postdoctoral grant from the Carlsberg Foundation.
2 James is discussing introspection in Chapter VII of *Principles of Psychology* ("The Methods and Snares of Psychology") under the subheading of "The Methods of Investigation".
3 The present discussion concerns introspection—(1) *not* phenomenology and (2) *not* introspectionism. (1) "The historical movement of phenomenology is the philosophical tradition launched in the first half of the 20th century by Edmund Husserl, Martin Heidegger, Maurice Merleau-Ponty, Jean-Paul Sartre, *et al.*" (Smith 2011). Comte's objections to introspection *preceded* phenomenology by nearly a century and were, obviously, not intended to attach to this philosophical project. Furthermore, it is worth remarking that the posited ambitions of phenomenology differ profoundly from what is normally sought by someone engaging in introspective self-observation. As Zahavi has put it, "classical phenomenology is not just another name for a kind of psychological self-observation; rather it must be appreciated as *a special form of transcendental philosophy* that seeks to reflect on the conditions of possibility of experience and cognition, and on the question of what conditions something must satisfy in order to count as 'real'" (Zahavi 2007, 77, italics added). In the present paper, we take no position on the philosophical prospects of the phenomenological project. (2) Introspectionism is a movement in psychology most closely associated with the work of Edward Bradford Titchener (1867–1927). Titchener was perhaps the leading experimental psychologist in the Anglo-American world during the first decade of the twentieth century. Boring, called him simply the "the dean of experimental psychology in America" (Boring 1927, 489). Titchener *claimed* to practice a form of experimental introspection that was *no less objective* than the observational practices in the natural sciences at the time—a point recently argued by Christopher Green (Green 2010). Yet, in reality, the form of "introspective" self-observation endorsed by Titchener was highly theory-laden and experimentally biased. One source of systematic bias was Titchener's view that the central aim of scientific psychological enquiry is the identification and the systematic inventorying of the least elements of the mental. As Titchener put it, the "primary aim of the experimental psychologist" is to "analyze the structure of mind; to ravel out the elemental processes from the tangle of

consciousness" (Titchener 1896, 450). To do this, one takes up "mental experiences, bit by bit, dividing and subdividing, until the division can go no further. When that point is reached ... a conscious element" has been found (ibid., 13). Going the other way, one must be able to say: "Give me my elements, and let me bring them together under the psychophysical conditions of mentality at large, and I will guarantee to show you the adult mind, as a structure, with no omissions and no superfluity" (ibid., 294). As this author has argued at length elsewhere, "experimental introspection," in the context of Titchenerian introspectionism, was a investigative process rather unlike what we today would recognize as introspection (see Beenfeldt 2011).

4 The translations of *Cours de philosophie positive* relied on in this paper are the Hackett edition (by Frederick Ferré) of the first two chapters of the *Cours*, the Harper edition (by Gertrud Lenzer), and Harriet Martineau's well-known translation of the complete work, here in the 1855 edition. The aim of the present paper is to consider Comte's timeless arguments against introspection as these were received by the wider intellectual community. Martineau's translation was an important conduit for this understanding, and thus this choice of translation (in addition to the two other supplementary translations) has been made. As a sign of the continuing relevance of this work, Martineau's translation (in two volumes) was part of the Cambridge Library Collection series, published in by Cambridge University Press in 2009.

5 In this work, Mill himself aims to show a close relationship between Comte's positivism and British associationism—including the work of David Hume, Thomas Brown, and his own father, James Mill (Mill 1961, 2–9).

6 Or, as we shall see, some localized region of the brain understood to be a sort of organ in itself.

7 Phrenology must be understood, however, not just as a theoretical doctrine but also as a popular *social movement*. See Wyhe 2004 for a detailed discussion.

8 Thomas Willis (1621–1675), British medical doctor and neuroanatomist, was an important precursor to Gall. It was a foundational assumption for Willis—as it later was for Gall, also—that there is a close correlation between the anatomical *structure*, the physiological *function*, and the mental operations of the brain. Finding however, by extensive comparative dissections, no structural differences adequate to account for the observed differences between rational men and irrational animals, Willis concludes that man is a two-souled creature with a material, sensitive soul and an immaterial, rational soul (see Bynum 1973 for a useful discussion of this). Gall, one might say, dispensed with Willis' rational soul, and largely relocated the structural seat of mental functions to the cerebral cortex (Bynum 1973, 467–68).

9 Many kinds of snails, in fact, have these kinds of eyestalks, also known as tentacles, which in comparative terms extend a great distance away from their head.

10 Nöe puts it as follows: "Consciousness isn't something that happens inside us: it is something we do, actively, in our dynamic interaction with the world around us. The brain—that particular bodily organ—is certainly critical to understanding how we work. But ... we need to look at the brain's job in relation to the larger nonbrain body and the environment in which we find ourselves" (Nöe 2008, 24).

11 As one commentator put it, rather strongly, "Descartes' antiskeptical productions are a later edition of the Augustinian and avail themselves of a comparable *introspective* mode of analysis" (Robinson 2008, 58).

12 The view of introspection as an "inner sense" should be distinguished from the related medieval theory of the *inner senses*—a neurophysiological theory derived from the work of Claudius Galen that "enjoyed wide acceptance in Europe from the fourth to the sixteenth century" (Kemp and Fletcher 1993, 559). According to this theory, specific areas in the brain (mainly the ventricles) in both animals and human beings are directly connected to the sensory organs and serve as storehouses for sensory content. The theory was destroyed by the revolutionary work in brain anatomy by Andreas Vasalius, whose *De Humani Corporis Fabrica* demonstrated the absence of the required direct sensory nerve access to the anterior ventricles (Kemp and Fletcher 1993, 566).

13 See Kuusela and Paul 2000 for an evaluative comparison, in the context of contemporary experimental work, of introspective protocols that are either concurrent or retrospective.

14 The books is a reprint of two essays that originally appeared in the *Westminster Review*.

15 Mill, in fact, did much to bring Comte's *Cours* to the attention of the English-speaking world (Raeder 2002, 59). "I had contributed more than any one else to make [Comte's] speculations known in England" (Mill 1989, 205). At first, Mill seemed almost to be a disciple of Comte (Mazlish 1975, 258).

16 This was not, of course, the only point where Mill disagreed with the *Cours* (see Lewisohn 1972).

17 Ryle thus rejects, in *The Concept of Mind*, the legitimacy of "introspection" (the noun), although he finds some use for "introspective" (the adjective). The latter term, he holds, is "ordinarily used in an innocuous sense to signify that someone pays more heed than usual to theoretical and practical problems about his own character, abilities, deficiencies and oddities; there is often the extra suggestion that the person is abnormally anxious about these matters" (Ryle 2000, 156).

18 As far as the nature of memory, this point is made well in Loftus 1996.

19 Reeves makes a similar point. In his estimate, the Comte-Mill break occurred because Mill insisted that "individuals could not be dissolved into society" (Reeves 2007, 199).

20 It should be emphasized that Comte had a *much* wider agenda than merely the objections to introspection that we have discussed here. As Mary Pickering has put it, Comte held that "the way to uncover the rules and operations of the mind was not by using pure logic and introspection but by observing the mind's work, its concrete products." "Comte sought to deflect attention away from the individual mind in order to concentrate on the exterior, collective facts of society" (Pickering 2006, 158–59). About *this* positive program, the present paper is completely silent.

References

Augustine (1986). *Confessions* (Pine-Coffin, translation). Penguin Books.

Augustine (1998). *Confessions* (Chadwick, translation). Oxford University Press.

Beenfeldt, C. (2011). *Introspection and the Scientific Study of the Mental: A Philosophical Analysis of Major Obstacles*. DPhil Thesis, Faculty of Philosophy, University of Oxford.

Bennett, M. R. and P. M. S. Hacker (2004). *Philosophical Foundations of Neuroscience*. Blackwell.

Bynum, W. F. (1973). "The Anatomical Method, Natural Theology, and the Functions of the Brain." *Isis* 64, no. 4.

Boring, E. G. (1927). "Edward Bradford Titchener: 1867–1927." *The American Journal of Psychology* 38, no. 4.

Boring, E. G. (1953). "A History of Introspection." *Psychological Bulletin* 50, no. 3.

Comte, A. (1855). *The Positive Philosophy of Auguste Comte* (Martineau, translation). Calvin Blanchard.

Comte, A. (1975). *Auguste Comte and Positivism: The Essential Writings* (Lenzer, ed. & translation). Harper.

Comte, A. (1988). *Introduction to Positive Philosophy* (Ferré, ed. & rev. translation). Hackett.

Cowan, N. (2001). "The Magical Number 4 in Short-Term Memory: A Reconsideration of Mental Storage Capacity." *Behavioral and Brain Sciences* 24, no. 1.

Descartes, R. (1993). *Discourse on Method and Meditations on First Philosophy* (Cress, translation). Hackett.

Gane, M. (2006). *Auguste Comte*. Key Sociologists Series (ed. Hamilton). Routledge.

Hatfield, G. (2005). "Introspective Evidence in Psychology." In Achinstein (ed.) *Scientific Evidence: Philosophical Theories and Applications*. Johns Hopkins University Press.

Hurlburt, R. T. and E. Schwitzgebel (2007). *Describing Inner Experience: Proponent Meets Skeptic*. MIT Press.

James, W. (1952). *The Principles of Psychology*. Encyclopædia Britannica.

Kemp, S. and G. J. O. Fletcher (1993). "The Medieval Theory of the Inner Senses." *The American Journal of Psychology*, 106, no. 4.

Kuusela, H. and P. Paul (2000). "A Comparison of Concurrent and Retrospective Verbal Protocol Analysis." *The American Journal of Psychology* 113, no. 3.

Lewisohn, D. (1972). "Mill and Comte on the Methods of Social Science." *Journal of the History of Ideas* 33, no. 2.

Loftus, E. F. (1996). *Eyewitness Testimony.* Harvard University Press.

Lyons, W. 1986. *The Disappearance of Introspection.* MIT Press.

Mazlish, B. (1975). *James and John Stuart Mill: Father and Son in the Nineteenth Century.* Basic Books.

Mill, J. S. (1961). *Auguste Comte and Positivism.* University of Michigan Press.

Mill, J. S. (1989). *Autobiography* (ed. Robson). Penguin Books.

Miller, G. A. (1956). "The Magical Number Seven, Plus or Minus Two: Some Limits on Our Capacity for Processing Information." *Psychological Review* 63, no. 2,

Neisser, U. (1976). *Cognition and Reality: Principles and Implications of Cognitive Psychology.* W. H. Freeman & Company.

Nöe, A. (2009). *Out of Our Heads: Why You Are Not Your Brain, and Other Lessons from the Biology of Consciousness.* Hill and Wang.

Pickering, M. (2006). *Auguste Comte: An Intellectual Biography, Volume 1.* Cambridge University Press.

Raeder, L. C. (2002). *John Stuart Mill and the Religion of Humanity.* University of Missouri Press.

Reeves, R. (2007). *John Stuart Mill: Victorian Firebrand.* Atlantic Books.

Robinson, D. N. (2008). *Consciousness and Mental Life.* Columbia University Press.

Ryle, G. (2000). *The Concept of Mind.* Penguin Books.

Scharff, R. C. (1989). "Mill's Misreading of Comte on 'Interior Observation'." *Journal of the History of Philosophy* 27, no. 4.

Scharff, R. C. (2002). *Comte after Positivism.* Cambridge University Press.

Siewert, C. (1998). *The Significance of Consciousness.* Princeton University Press.

Titchener, E. B. (1896). *An Outline of Psychology.* Macmillan.

Tresch, J. (2011). Review of "Mary Pickering, Auguste Comte: An Intellectual Biography." *Journal of Modern History* 83, no. 3.

Wilson, F. (1991). Mill and Comte on the Method of Introspection. *Journal of the History of the Behavioral Sciences* 27, no. 2.

Smith, D. W. (2011). Phenomenology. *The Stanford Encyclopedia of Philosophy* (Zelta, E. N, ed.). http://plato.stanford.edu/archives/fall2011/entries/phenomenology

Wyhe, John van. (2004). *Phrenology and the Origins of Victorian Scientific Naturalism.* Ashgate.

Zahavi, D. (2007). Subjectivity and the First-Person Perspective. *The Southern Journal of Philosophy*, vol. XLV.

AGAMBEN. NAKED LIFE AND NUDITY

LARS ÖSTMAN

University of Copenhagen

...non ti ricordi che tutte e due siamo nate dalla Caducità?
– Leopardi, Dialogo della Moda e della Morte

Trachtet am ersten nach Nahrung und Kleidung,
so wird euch das Reich Gottes von selbst zufallen.
– Hegel, An Knebel, 30 August 1807

Abstract

The Italian thinker Giorgio Agamben has achieved large international recognition since his first book in the *homo sacer*-project, *Homo sacer. Il potere sovrano e la nuda vita*, was published in 1995. The project's basic aim is to try and understand the fundamental relation between man and power, politics and theology, which Agamben gives the name biopolitics. Such a politics, Agamben writes in the introduction, is the very fundamental element of Western metaphysics, "because it occupies the threshold in which the articulation between the living and logos is accomplished."[1] With relentless stringency scholars and researchers have analysed Agamben's perhaps most famous concept, naked life, and related it to the history of religion, philosophy of law etc. The philosopher himself never thought that his term naked life would achieve such fame, as he said at a small conference at Iuav.[2] However, what has been given less attention, if any, is the most obvious part in that concept: nudity. This holds the key, nonetheless, to understand Agamben's thinking, because nudity is that very threshold holding together, as well as separating, life and logos, man and animal. Perhaps this is one of the reasons, if not needs, for Agamben writing a book with the telling title: *Nudità*.

Centre in the present article is to discuss Agamben's concept of nudity alongside that of naked life in thematizing the term shame which is central in this regard.³ Furthermore, the attempt to argue in favour of a conceptual use of the metaphor—naked life—shall also be unfolded.

Naked Life as Citation

In Agamben's *homo sacer*-project, the term naked is part of one of Agamben's most famous concepts: naked life. In the first book of this project *homo sacer* (sacred man) is derived by way of a citation from the Roman grammarian Festus' *De verborum significatu* (On the Meaning of Words).⁴

Already in his introduction Agamben quotes Festus when he writes that when a man is produced as naked life he is instantly transformed into "the life of *homo sacer* (sacred man) who may be killed and yet not sacrificed."⁵ Agamben hereby follows a literary methodology of citation in Western tradition from the Middle Ages to Dante and, most of all, to Walter Benjamin.⁶ Agamben's philosophical analysis of (Western) ontology places itself in the slipstream of Benjamin's strategy from his *Passagen-Werk* where the proclamation "to write history signifies *quoting* history" suggests such a medieval praxis.⁷ In Agamben the citation becomes testimony and the author, Agamben himself, witness. The citation (testimony) becomes a kind of literary resurrection whose "life" now consists in being commented, in being witnessed. It is in this light we can read the citations from the surviving *Muselmänner*, the witnesses, which ends *Quel che resta di Auschwitz*. The citation as voice (of the *auctor*) is that which remains and, it its own turn, is in need of comment.

Auctoritas also seems to be carrying a juridical connotation, as the verb *cito* also signifies to be called to justice, to call the witness to present himself in court as *auctor*. "*Auctor* is," Baroncini writes, "precisely, the *testis* [witness] who can guarantee the authenticity of the affirmations of others, like a philosopher or a poet who assumes an exemplary value for his dignity and force of persuasion."⁸ However, Agamben writes in *Stanze*, for the Middle Ages there is not, in fact, any possibility of citing a text in the modern sense of the word, instead "the medieval texts are contained as citations within the *antiqui auctores* (which explains, amongst other things, the medieval penchant for the gloss as a literary form)."[9] The gloss (gr. *glôssa*; lat. *glossa*), defined by any standard dictionary, is an explanation, interpretation or a comment to a difficult or foreign word.[10] Naturally, the *glossa* often appears in relation to a citation as the author's worth as *auctor* truly is measured here. Because, the citation is used "to prove and support what is new."[11] It is precisely the *glossa* defined as commentary praxis which holds the key to Agamben's method. Agamben is a reader, a commentator and his texts are written as glosses in the margin of history very much like Benjamin imagined such a work.[12]

Naked life is just such a gloss to Festus' *homo sacer*. Nonetheless, its explanatory method is by way of a poetic metaphor. And yet, Agamben insists, it is a technical term. To Agamben this is exactly what defines thinking. Terminology, Agamben states in *Che cos'è un dispositivo?*, "is the poetic moment of thinking."[13] By using a poetical or, at least, metaphorical formulation, one could say that naked life is a *homo sacer* who has been stripped of his rights. Naked life becomes Agamben's "translation" or modern comment to Festus' *homo sacer*. Where Festus underlines an almost democratic principle behind the *homo sacer* ("*At homo sacer est, quem populus iudicavit ob maleficum*"[14]), Agamben must interpret it anew to make it correspond with the contemporary meaning of sacred. Sacred now denotes sovereign violence which does not belong to sacrificial ideology, like in Antiquity, since it signifies a man who may not be sacrificed.[15] "The meaning of the term sacred in our culture," Agamben concludes, "continues the semantical history of *homo sacer* and not that of the sacrifice [...]."[16] It does not concern religion or politics but biopolitics. Agamben's naked life becomes a secularised version of Festus' *homo sacer* by way of letting the glossology operate as a philosophical comment. What was once divine (*homo sacer*) now *also* operates in the political (naked life).[17] Many such examples relying on this Agambian definition of naked life as exposed to sovereign violence can be given: the witch, the unclean and, of course, the Jew in the Third Reich who to Agamben remain the constant paradigm in the *homo sacer*-project. Common to all is that they live on a "threshold of indifference" between *physis* and *nómos*, land and city, man and animal.[18] With his term naked life Agamben could be said to try and explain this paradoxical life, which has been with us from the start of the philosophical tradition—at least since Aristotle's *Politica*:

> But he who is unable to live in a society (*koinôneîn*), or who has no need because he is sufficient for himself, must be either a beast (*thêrion*) or a god (*thêos*): he is no part of the state (*póleôs*).[19]

Agamben's political thinking is, most of all, a reflection on biopolitics. The concept was introduced by Michel Foucault and, indeed, Agamben does share many of Foucault's methodological strategies in this regard.[20] He even sees his work as "very close to that of Foucault."[21] The affinity is seen again in his grand œuvre, *Il Regno e la Gloria*, locating itself "in the wake of Michel Foucault's investigations."[22] However, as much as the two authorships share basic methodologies, they differ when it comes to concrete fields of (historical) philosophical analysis. Where biopolitics to Foucault concerns the institutionalisation of biological facts into the realms of politics mainly in the 18th century, Agamben's interests are founded in the suspension of the institution and of Law as such. He concerns himself with thresholds of indifference, i.e. states of exception.[23] This directs Agamben's investigations into jurisprudence and theology, "the two he [Foucault] had left out."[24] More than a historical hypothesis and enterprise, like Foucault's, Agamben's concern a political ontology trying to grasp the root of politics—having, of course, a historical outset. In other words, where Foucault's ideas concern an analysis of historical events, Agamben's try to reveal and analyse history in the form of the paradigm—for instance Auschwitz—in examining the ontology of politics.[25]

Naked Life and Shame

"Every subjectification," Agamben said at a lecture in 2007 at the Iuav University, "is a de-subjectification." This is seen, in particular, when it comes to the thematic of shame. In *Quel che resta di Auschwitz*, the statement is mentioned repeatedly with only little variation. In the book, with De La Durantaye's words, "the focus is not on how the *space* of the camp is a figure for the "biopolitical" spaces of modern city, as it was in [the first] *Homo Sacer*, but instead on bearing witness to the life lived there."[26] And such a witnessing of lived life in Auschwitz—or in any camp—has, precisely, shame at its centre.

The shame experienced by the survivors of the Third Reich extermination politics is often treated in the witness literature. What Agamben holds against much of this kind of literature is that it—like Wiesel's "I'm alive, therefore I'm guilty"—reproduces the dogmas of Judaism and Christianity.[27] Wiesel's position, of course, leads the thoughts to back to the Fall, i.e. to the myth that man as such from the first moment in time bears a guilt from which he cannot run but only be redeemed by God, and redressed in the clothes of His eternal glory. The witness literature most of all resembles confession literature of which St. Augustine and his *Confessiones* together form the key example.

> [...] the formation of Western subjectivity, together both cleaved and yet master and secure of itself, has since centuries been inseparable from the action of the penitential dispositive where a new I is constructed through the negation and, at the same time, the assumption of the old one.[28]

To Levi, Wiesel and other writers of witness literature the task was, just as it had been for the repentant Augustine, to describe a new ethics. Or, as one could perhaps say when it comes to the witness literature of the Nazi camp, the lack of ethics.

In this regard, Agamben's attempt in *Quel che resta di Auschwitz* is another one. Agamben examines the Auschwitz-ethics on its ontological level. To Agamben this means to not try and develop a new theory of ethics based on the testimonies from the surviving witnesses. Readers of his book on Auschwitz, Agamben writes, will find "little new when it comes to the testimonies from the survivors."[29] The idea, instead, is to ask what it takes for something like ethics to take place. How and why can we say that ethics is something akin to an "ontological happening"? The reason, for Agamben, is that the ontology of ethics lies within the possibility of shame to take place. Shame reveals itself on the threshold of subjectification and de-subjectification. Therefore, De La Durantaye writes, "what we should note is that Agamben examines shame as an extending beyond the empirical coordinates of any specific act or omission."[30] Shame is examined as an ontological existential, and as the gate to ethics as such.

When it comes to shame, the sadomasochist affair is enlightening. If the sadist and the masochist were discovered in the heat of their lust, shame would not belong to either one of them. The shame would blush scarlet on their cheeks, but derive from neither one of them: "subjectification and de-subjectification circulates incessantly between the two poles without really belonging to anyone."[31] They mutually dress and re-dress each other in dignity, and if their shame should be revealed it would equally involve both of them. Opposite of the sadomasochist incident is the situation between the SS and the inmate in the camp. The continuous Nazi subjectification—or creation—of *the* German Aryan (the highest goal for the thousand-year reign) has its de-subjectification, its counterpart, in the naked life of the *Muselmann*, "not only and not so much a limit between life and death; he signifies, rather, the threshold between man and no-man."[32] The *Muselmann* is the limit of the Nazi biopolitical caesuras.[33] The construction of the German, hence, requires that he is established over and over again with a constant reference: the Un-german. In the same sense, so it seems, that the sadist and the masochist need each other. However, unlike the sadomasochist orgy, the SS and the *Muselmann* never change poles—it does seem rather unlikely that the *Muselmann* would desire the SS like the sadist desires his masochistic "better half." Instead, the two poles remain absolute and with one single origin.

The extreme case of this is found in the French poet and author Robert Antelme's example from his *L'espèce humaine* (1947), which Agamben treats in this book on Auschwitz. It concerns a young Italian student randomly chosen by the SS who looks for someone, anyone, to kill:

> An SS calls out again. *'Du komme hier'*. Another Italian steps forward. It is a student from Bologna. I know him, and I look at him noticing that his face has turned pink. I looked at him closely, and I still have that astonishing blush before my eyes. He is ashamed, and does not know what to do with his hands.... He turned pink right after that SS said to him, *'Du komme hier!'* He looked around himself before blushing, but it really was him they wanted and, at the moment when he no longer doubted, he turned pink.[34]

Agamben asks why this young Italian student felt ashamed. He was simply chosen. That is all. Nothing else happened. He does not tell or show anything private or embarrassing. He has not done anything wrong and yet he blushed; yet he felt ashamed. What, in the personal history of this young man could be revealed in those few seconds? In his *De l'évasion*, which Agamben brings into the analysis, the French philosopher, Emmanuel Levinas, reflects on the concept of shame. Shame, Agamben is taught by Levinas, is that from which we cannot escape. Shame is most of all what constitutes the human being resembling a Heideggerian *Existenziale*.[35] It is when reflecting on Levinas' analysis of shame together with the example of the young Italian student that the example of nudity appears:If nudity results in us being ashamed, it is because we cannot hide that which we would prefer to hide from the glance of the eye. Because, the unrestrainable impulse of escaping from oneself is encountered by an equal certain impossibility of evasion.[36]

Agamben follows his insight from Levinas back to his master, Heidegger. In his course on Parmenides he had described shame (*aidòs*) as "a fundamental word in authentic Greekness," and this to such a degree that Heidegger the page after even wrote that "Being itself carries shame with it, the shame of being."[37] Shame is that moment in time where the subject becomes aware of the fact that he is subject (-ed); when the subject realises that he is re-veiled as such in a world, i.e. to the Other. Shame is the moment in time where a subject becomes aware not only that he sees but even that he is seen. Not only does he know he is a subject but, far more important, he realises the fact that his subjectivity—which up until this point had been his and his alone—is exposed to the Other and world. Shame is each and every moment in life when subjectivity is de-subjectified. Shame has ontological character.[38] Following Heidegger, one could say that when the subject renders account that his being is a being-in-the-world then he, at the same time, becomes a shameful being.[39] Shame is not a state, something into which we are born but an event, something which comes into being:

> In shame, thus, the subject has no other contents than his own de-subjectification. He has become witness of his own disorder, his own fall as subject. This double movement, both subjectification and de-subjectification, is shame.[40]

If we now turn to the example with the young Italian student, a decisive ethical—and political—ontological element can be found. Shame's relation to nudity conditions the very revelation of naked life and, therefore, of sovereign power. This is the dialectics of subjectification / de-subjectification. Whenever there is sovereign power controlling shame (that which makes humanity human), there is naked life. The dialectics which worked in the sadomasochist *séance* letting, in the end, dignity flow between the two poles, does not exist here. Nudity turns into shame, the I into sovereign (the SS), the Other into naked life (the young Italian student). Not to recognise the shame in another human being, is to produce oneself as sovereign and the Other as naked life, a life that may, in the end, be killed but not sacrificed.

In the classical Greek tradition, in which Heidegger believed shame (*aidòs*) to be a fundamental word, another example is found where it is seen that sovereign is the one controlling and governing shame. In the passage concerning the older history of the Kingdom of Lydia, Herodotus writes of Gyges. His lord, King Candaules, has ordered Gyges, who is a mere slave, to hide behind the king's bedroom door so that he can see the naked queen and be sure of the fact (which he himself has no wish of) that Candaules' wife really is the most beautiful woman of all. The loyal Gyges does as he is told but gives, nonetheless, as reason for his unwillingness a most interesting reflection: "[…] with the clothes by which a woman undresses herself, she undresses even her shame."[41] The queen discovers the hiding Gyges but is, nonetheless, not ashamed. She restrains herself and quickly realises that her husband, King Candaules, voluntarily has put her in this shameful situation of being seen naked—even by a slave. Naturally for a Greek mentality she forces Gyges to kill her husband, the king and his lord as revenge or else the queen will tell in public that Gyges has seen what is illegal: another man's naked wife and therefore that shame has left the private sphere and expanded beyond its borders into the city and the realms of politics. Gyges' reward will, of course, be the throne and the queen herself. Like before, Gyges obeys. He kills King Candaules and wins both queen and kingdom.

How is a dressed body naked—that is ashamed—and, vice versa, a naked body dressed—that is not ashamed? The first can be said in the case of the young Italian student, the second of King Candaules' queen. But what, if Agamben's idea of a kind of dialectics is at stake, is the paradigm for a form of life where shame should present itself but does not? The *locus classicus* for such a "dressed nakedness" is the myth of Adam and Eve in The Garden of Eden.

Nudity and Shame

Next time Agamben takes up the question of shame is in *Nudità*. In this book Agamben continues his analysis from *Quel che resta di Auschwitz* but now goes to the philological and textual root of the problem: the nudity of Adam and Eve in The Garden of Eden and, hence, shame and the beginning of ethics. In *Nudità* Agamben could be said to present a clearer answer as to why it is methodological meaningful to use the term naked life, i.e. to qualify his use of a metaphor as a concept. The young Italian student who was undressed of his humanity, realising his own de-subjectification and therefore shame, must have, in one way or the other if Agamben is to be true to his "conceptual metaphoric" idea of nudity, something in common with Adam and Eve who were "both naked, the man and his wife, and were not ashamed."[42] The question of shame seems to be the question of human nature.

Common to Agamben's style and method, which we mentioned above, a citation lies at the ground for the analysis: "And the eyes of them both were opened, and they knew that they were naked (*Gen.* 3,7)."[43] Our ancestral prototypes quickly made clothes to cover their nakedness although they were, so it seems, just as naked before. Wandering around in The Garden of Eden, Adam and Eve are surveyed by God who controls his empire. Do his creations sin or can they, in the end, uphold His divine Law? Following Agamben's idea of shame as the moment in time where subjectivity is constituted by way of the process subjectification/de-subjectification, in The Garden of Eden, thus, no subjectivity exists. Shame cannot take place. At centre is not an epistemological issue; the interesting question is not whether they knew of their nudity or not.[44] Such a question is meaningless. Because, in The Garden of Eden (which in the Christian tradition later will be interpreted as Paradise) knowledge has no purpose, neither need nor meaning and therefore no existence.

However, contrary to what the Biblical text clearly states, according to the theologians Adam and his wife were not really naked, Agamben explains. Because, "they were covered by a clothes of grace which suited them as a glorious clothes."[45] The sygtagm "glorious clothes" is here decisive. Agamben quickly notes that it is Augustine who in his *De civitate dei* uses this formulation. Here, the Christian philosopher speaks about the paradisiacal "clothes" as precisely such an *indumentum gratiae* (clothing in grace).

> But, precisely therefore, this also means that its addition in origin has constituted human corporeity as "nude" and that its sub-

traction always returns to show it like this.[...] Therefore Adam is "dressed" in supernatural justice, in innocence and in immortality, because only these clothes attribute him his dignity and the human nature as his obscure carrier: the "naked" corporeity.[46]

Our paradisiacal ancestors, we read in Agamben's interpretation of the Biblical passage, are dressed by the grace of God, i.e. sovereign power. This grace fits them like a clothes. At the same time, it dresses them in dignity because nudity does not appear. They are not ashamed. Following this analysis, the moment where nudity occurs and shame takes place, thus letting the process subjectification/de-subjectification begin, is at the moment of the Fall. The clothes of grace as supernatural justice, innocence and immortality do no longer suit the paradisiacal citizens. Instead, they must make clothes to cover their natural injustice, guilt and mortality. Their bodies have, simply, changed after the Fall. It is no longer a gracious and glorious body, but a sinful one.

> This means that nudity is presented to our ancestors in the earthly Paradise in only two instances: a first time in the presumably very short interval between the perception of nudity and the confection of loincloths and, a second time, when they undress themselves from the fig leaves to wear garments of skin. Also in these brief moments nudity, so to say, is only presented negatively as the privation of the clothes of grace and as a foretoken of the splendid clothes of glory which the blessed will receive in Paradise.[47]

This incident is in the Old Testament myth of Adam and Eve the reason why a re-dressing by sovereign power is necessary. And, furthermore, the first real "historical" beings in the West always long for the re-dressing in the divine clothes of glory and grace they once wore. The separation between Law and man is always longed to be re-established. Adam's disobedience in The Garden of Eden rapidly leads to the problem of nudity and human clothes and therefore shame.[48] The artistic rendering on some reliquaries, e.g. in the collegiate church of Saint Isidoro in Lyon like Agamben mentions, show this longing. It pictures the violence of the divine fashion, showing God forcing the clothes upon Eve who "resists the divine violence with all energy."[49] Let us try to follow these considerations and compare it with our analysis of naked life we conducted above.

In his *Theologie des Kleides* from 1934, the German, Catholic theologian Erik Peterson examined the German saying: "Kleider machen Leute."[50] The title as well as its date of publication are interesting. It was the year after the most well known democratic election in the West. Hitler could now have the finest uniforms delivered to his most outstanding officers, those in the SS, by Hugo Boss.[51] Even Mercedes, Hitler favourite car mark, has a legend of beauty attached to its enterprise: the Austrian-Hungarian dealer of Daimler's cars, Emil Jellinek, found his own daughter, Mercedes, so heavenly beautiful that Daimler's new invention could bear no other name. The elegant clothes of the SS are in the most fundamental opposition to the "clothes" of the *Muselmann*, the paradigmatic life in a camp. What is it that turns their clothes into those of the living dead, grave clothes and the SS clothes into that of life, pomp and circumstance? In other words, how far may one stretch Peterson's aphorism which simply seems to be an interpretation of the Fall since it really is clothes (or the lack of them) that define Adam and Eve?

The difference between the "*Lichtkleid*" of the SS uniform and the rags of the *Muselmann* almost depositions the aesthetic dispositive of Christ's clothes of resurrection distancing themselves from the clothes of mortality. Like the SS wore the silver skull brooch, as if death in one way or the other was defeated or, at least, controlled, so the Jew wore his Star of David, which culminated in the *Muselmann*: the living symbol of a naked life that may be killed and yet not sacrificed. As Agamben stresses in his archaeology of glory, its Judeo-Christian terms—the frame of reference for the later part of the *homo sacer*-project—*doxa*, *kâbod* and *gloria*, are not relative to the beautiful but to power.[52] Of course, Greeks and Romans had goddesses for beauty too, but it was the gods of art that were powerful. The purpose of the SS-uniform, and with Nazi aesthetics in general, is not to be beautiful but to correlate itself with power. The SS uniform, like Adam's and Eve's divine clothes, becomes the clothes of grace, of supernatural justice and immortality. Like Adam and Eve's worldly clothes, the Star of David is a fashion signifying sure death. In his living Hell the *Muselmann* has been stripped of dignity, grace, and glory like of a clothes leaving him with only a naked life. And,

Agamben reminds us, "according to Christian theology there is one legal institution alone which does not know of neither interruption nor end: hell."⁵³

Peterson does therefore not only speak of Adam and Eve, but of the caesura in man himself between human and non-human:

> Like clothes presupposes the body it is supposed to cover, thus, grace presupposes the nature it has to cover with glory. This is why the supernatural grace suits the human being in Paradise like a clothes. *The human being is created without clothes* – this means that he had a nature of his own, different from the divine one – *but he has been created in this absence of clothes to be redressed in the supernatural clothes of glory.*⁵⁴

Agamben can then easily conclude right after: "The problem of nudity is, hence, the problem of human nature in its relation with grace."⁵⁵ In order to be a historical being man needs the clothes of divine Law and glory. Whatever is truly human, which Peterson calls nature, cannot be set free nor seen but must be controlled and dressed by a sovereign. This can either be done, as was the case for Adam and Eve, by way of covering this (sinful) nature with Law itself, of which clothes become a symbol. Or, as in the Third Reich, it can be done by eliminating such a nature (the Ungerman: the communist, the homosexual, the Jew etc.) which cannot live in the realms of the reign. The outcome is the same: naked life will not appear within the city walls.⁵⁶

In the Biblical account where the transition from non-humanity to humanity has the form of a transition from The Garden of Eden (non-humanity) to the world (humanity), it concerns the separation between man and Law (an anti-biopolitics).⁵⁷ The Nazi strategy is opposite. There is no separation between man and Law in the Third Reich, as was the outcome of the Fall. It is important to not forget that the juridical reference to *Lebensraum* in the political-juridical tradition refers to neither *terra* nor *imperium* but *corpus*.⁵⁸ Just as in The Garden of Eden, between sovereign (Hitler) and citizen (*Volk*) existed an identity and a harmony. To both sovereignties the reference is to the myth of an original nature, a naked corporeity, a naked life which need grace and glory:

Like the political mythologeme of *homo sacer*, in which an unclean, sacred and therefore one that may be killed, presupposes a naked life which has been produced only from that, in this way the naked corporeity of human nature is merely the opaque presupposition of such an originary and luminous supplement which is the clothes of grace. Hidden by these, the naked corporeity reemerges for the eye when the caesura of sin anew separates nature and grace, nudity and clothes. (Agamben 2009, 95)

Agamben's latest book, *Altissima povertà*, has its starting point in the Christian tradition similar to what *Nudità* had. Because, it is certainly true, Agamben writes, that creation and salvation do define the two poles of divine action and, likewise, "if it is true that God is the space in which human beings consider their decisive problems they also consider human action."[59] In *Altissima povertà*, the thematic veil/unveil plays a significant role once again. Peterson's aphorism, "Kleider machen Leute," in which we found a parallel to the SS and Nazi aesthetics is, perhaps not surprising given Agamben's theme in the book, also approached. In this regard, the clothes of the monk become paradigmatic serving as Agamben's attempt to deactivate this intimacy between aesthetics and power. The adagio "clothes do not make the monk" is in strict opposition to "Kleider machen Leute."[60] To cancel the difference between life (Leute) and language (Kleider), unveil and veil is to insist *"on the missing articulation between the living and the logos."*[61] Neither Hell nor Paradise but the Open is Agamben's idea of a "political redemption," and this opening of human world is especially an opening of the conflict between veil and unveil.[62] This idea continues to have Heidegger as its presupposition. As Heidegger rhetorically asks in *Sein und Zeit*:

Ist das Dasein als geworfenes In-der-Welt-sein nicht gerade zunächst in die Öffentlichkeit des Man geworfen? Und was bedeutet diese Öffentlichkeit anderes als die spezifische *Erschlossenheit* des Man?[63]

Notes

1 Agamben (1995, 11).
2 Conference held at Iuav- università di Venezia, Spring 2007.
3 In the following, the analysis of the witness and the testimony which in Agamben's *Quel che resta di Auschwitz* is also tied to shame shall not occupy me. This has been amply analysed by others (cf. e.g. Mills, in: Norris (2005, 198–221); Su Rasmussen, in: Bolt and Lund Pedersen (2005, 125–31). In the following all translations are my own unless otherwise indicated, sharp parentheses, [], indicate my insertions in the text. References to Agamben's א-sections are indicated in the reference as well (I have elsewhere tried to explain the purpose of such sections (cf. Östman [2012], 136–40)).
4 Agamben (1995, 79).
5 Agamben (1995, 11). This sentence, or variation of it, is mentioned throughout the book.
6 Only what methodological is most necessary for an understanding of the present article's scope will be treated in the following. Agamben's (literary) method and the complex thematics of the citation requires an autonomous work.
7 Benjamin (1972–1999, V,1, 595).
8 Baroncini (2002, 153). In 2002 the journal *Leitmotiv* devoted a whole theme issue to citation. Thinking on Agamben's work in philosophy of literature, interesting in the present context, besides Baroncini's, is the article of Scaramuzza (2002).
9 Agamben (1977, 86).
10 Cf. Lewis and Short or *Oxford English Dictionary*.
11 Baroncini (2002, 153).
12 Benjamin (1972–1999, vol. I, 2, 690–708).
Agamben has elsewhere used the term gloss, which is a technical one, and associated it with that of the margin: "Glosse in margine ai Commentari sulla societa della spettacolo," in: Agamben (1996, 60–73). Sorabji ([1990]: 1–27) gives some reflections on the Ancient commentary tradition.
13 Agamben (2006, 5).
14 Festus cit in: Agamben (1995, 79) ("*Homo sacer* is he whom the people has convicted for a crime").
15 Agamben (1995, 126).
16 Agamben (1995, 126).
17 Cf. Agamben (2005, 87f.).
18 Agamben (1995, 91; 117).
19 Aristotle, *Pol*, 1253a27.
20 Agamben's book on method is, most of all, based on what he calls a Benjaminian interpreta-

tion of the methodology of Foucault (Agamben [2008]: 7). This is especially true for the first and third chapter of the book dealing with the paradigm and (philosophical) archaeology.
21 Sacco (2004).
22 Agamben (2007, 9).
23 Therefore Agamben can write that "it is not possible to inscribe the analysis of the camp in the open trails of Foucault's works, in *Histoire de la folie* and *Surveiller et punir*. The camp as the absolute space of exception is topologically different from a simple space of confinement" (Agamben [1995]: 23–24). The state of exception is, Agamben writes in his book devoted to the matter in question, "this no man's land between public law and political fact, and between juridical order and life" (Agamben [2003]: 10).
24 Sacco (2004).
25 For a longer discussion of the relation between Foucault and Agamben, cf: Patton, in: Calarco and DeCaroli (2007, 203–18); in his lectures at College de France, especially from 1976–1980, Foucault commences his study of biopolitics and the concepts most related to that, biopower. Cf. esp. Foucault (1976, 216–20); (1977–1978, 3–31, 91–118).
26 De La Durantaye (2009, 248).
27 Agamben (1998, 83).
28 Agamben (2006, 29f.).
29 Agamben (1998, 9).
30 De La Durantaye (2009, 278).
31 Agamben (1998, 100).
32 Agamben (1998, 5).
33 Agamben (1998, 79).
34 Agamben (1998, 95).
35 Heidegger (1927, §9, 44f.).
36 Agamben (1998, 96).
37 Heidegger cited in Agamben (1998, 98).
38 Agamben (1998, 98).
39 Agamben (1998, 104). "*In-Sein ist demnach der formale existenziale Ausdruck des Seins des Daseins, das die wesenhafte Verfassung des In-der-Welt-seins hat*" (Heidegger [1927]: §12, 54).
40 Agamben (1998, 97).
41 Herodotus, book 1,6–7.
42 Bible, *Gen.*2,25. LXX and Vulgata respectively render naked as *gymnos* and *nudo* and shame, in the verbal form as *aìschynô* and *erubusco*.
43 Agamben (2009, 85).
44 Agamben (2009, 85).

45 Agamben (2009, 85).
46 Agamben (2009, 93).
47 Agamben (2009, 86f.).
48 For a treatment of Adam's disobedience, cf: Coccia (2008).
49 Agamben (2009, 90).
50 Peterson (1934, 12).
51 Cf. e.g. Wivel (2008).
52 Agamben (2007, 219; 223).
53 Agamben (2010, 18).
54 Peterson (1934), cited in Agamben (2009, 89–90).
55 Agamben (2009, 90).
56 The praxis of the Catholic church is, in this regard, examplary: following the prediction in the Gospels, when all Jews are christianised Paradise will come and the Lord present himself. With relentless logic, the Vatican and Pio XII saw the possibility to collaborate with the Third Reich in the extermination of the Italian Jews which on October 16, 1943 came to the deportation of nearly all Roman Jews. Converted or eliminated, the result remains the same: the Jews do no longer exist (cf. Brechenmacher [2005]: 218–23).
57 Cf. Coccia (2008, 35f.).
58 "(…) even when *corpus* becomes the central metaphor for the political community in *Leviathan* or in *The Social Contract*, it always maintains a close relation to naked life" (Agamben [1995]: 138).
59 Agamben (2009, 11).
60 Agamben (2011, 27)
61 Agamben (1998, 125f.)
62 Agamben (2002, 65).
63 Heidegger (1927, §34, 167 (my italics). For an interpretation of Christian features of Heidegger's thinking cf. Fischer and von Herrmann (ed.) (2007). Concerning *Dasein* as 'geworfenes', cf. Ringleben, in Fischer and von Herrmann (ed.) (2007, 219–45).

References

Agamben, Giorgio (2011). *Altissima povertà. Regole monastiche e forma di vita. Homo sacer IV,1*, Neri Pozza, Vicenza.

Agamben, Giorgio (2010). *La Chiesa e il Regno*, Nottetempo, Rome.

Agamben, Giorgio (2009). *Nudità*, Nottetempo, Rome.

Agamben, Giorgio (2008). *Signatura rerum. Sul metodo*, Bollati Boringhieri, Torino.

Agamben, Giorgio (2007). *Il Regno e la Gloria. Per una genealogia teologica dell'economia e del governo. Homo sacer, II, 2*, Neri Pozza, Rome.

Agamben, Giorgio (2005). *Profanazioni*, Nottetempo, Rome.

Agamben, Giorgio (2006). *Che cos'è un dispositivo ?* Nottetempo, Rome.

Agamben, Giorgio (2003). *Stato di eccezione*. Homo sacer, II, i, Bollati Boringhieri, Torino 2004.

Agamben, Giorgio (2002). *L'Aperto. L'uomo e l'animale*, Bollati Boringhieri, Torino 2003.

Agamben, Giorgio (1998). *Quel che resta da Auschwitz. L'archivio e il testimone (Homo sacer III)*, Bollati Boringhieri, Torino 2005.

Agamben, Giorgio (1995). Homo sacer. *Il potere sovrano e la nuda vita*, Einaudi, Torino 2005.

Agamben, Giorgio (1977). *Stanze. La parola e il fantasma nelle cultura occidentale*, Einaudi, Torino 2006.

Aristotle, *Politica*, in: www.perseus.tufts.edu, trans: Benjamin Jowett, *Politics*, Batoche Book, Kitchener, 1999.

Baroncini, Daniele (2002). "Citazione e memoria classica in Dante," in: *Leitmotiv*, no. 2 (www.ledoline.it/leitmotiv/).

Benjamin, Walter (1972–1999). "Das Passagen-Werk" in: Id. Tiedemann and Schwäppenhäuser (ed.) *Gesammelte Werke*, Frankfurt am Main, vol. V, 1 pp. 1–654.

Benjamin, Walter (1972–1999). "Über den Begriff der Geschichte" in: Id. Tiedemann and Schwäppenhäuser (ed.), *Gesammelte Werke*, Frankfurt am Main, vol. I, 2, pp. 690–708.

Bibles. *King James Version*, *Septuaginta* (LXX), *Vulgata*, available at: www.biblegateway.com

Brechenbacher, Thomas (2005). *Der Vatikan und die Juden. Geschichte einer unheiligen Beziehung*. C.H. Bech, München.

Calarco, Matthew and Steven DeCaroli (2007). *Giorgio Agamben. Sovereignty and Life*. Stanford: Stanford University Press.

Coccia, Emanuele (2008). "'Inobedientia'. Il peccato di Adamo e l'antropologia giudaico-cristiana." *Filosofia Politica*, XXII, no. 1 (April).

De La Durantaye, Leland (2009). *Giorgio Agamben: A Critical Introduction*. Stanford: Stanford University Press.

Fischer, Norbert and Friedrich-Wilhelm von Herrmann (ed.) (2007). *Heidegger und die christliche Tradition. Annäherungen an ein schwieriges Thema*, Feliz Meiner, Hamburg.

Foucault, Michel (1976). *"Il faut défendre la société."* Cours au Collège de France 1976, Seuil/Gallimard, 1997.

Foucault, Michel (1977–1978). *Sécurité, territoire, population*, Cours au Collège de France, Seuil/Gallimard, 2004.

Herodotus. *The Histories of Herodotus*, trans. C. E. Godley, Harvard University Press, 1920.

Heidegger, Martin (1927). *Sein und Zeit*, Max Niemeyer, 11. Aufl., Tübingen 1967.

Levi, Neil and Michael Rothberg (2004). "Auschwitz and the Remains of Theory: Towards an Ethics of the Borderland." *Symploke* 11, no. 1–2: 23–38.

Norris, Andrew (ed.) (2005). *Politics, Metaphysics, and Death. Essays on Giorgio Agamben's Homo Sacer*, Duke University, Durham/London.

Östman, Lars (2012). *Giorgio Agamben: Nøgenhed*. Frederiksberg: Forlaget Anis.

Peterson, Erik (1994 [1934]). "Theologie des Kleides." In *Ausgewählte Schriften* I. Echter Verlag, Würzburg.

Sacco, Gian-Luca (2004). "A Giorgio Agamben: dalla teologia politica alla teologia economica," in: *Scuola superiore dell'economia e delle finanze*, n.4, a.I, juni-juli 2004, reprinted at *La voce di Fiore* (29 September 2006: http://www.lavocedifiore.org/SPIP/article.php3?id_article=1209).

Scaramuzza, Gabriele (2002). "Citazione come oblio." *Leitmotiv*, no.1 (www.ledoline.it/leitmotiv/)

Sorabji, Richard (1990) (ed.). "The Ancient Commentators on Aristotle." In *Aristotle Transformed: The Ancient Commentators and Their Influence*. Cornell University Press, New York, pp. 1–27.

Wivel, Peter (2008). *Modeimperium leverede uniformer til SS* (kronik), in: *Politiken*, 31 August 2008.

A CRITIQUE OF LAURENCE BONJOUR'S CENTRAL ARGUMENTS FOR A PRIORI FALLIBILISM

Nikolaj Nottelmann

University of Southern Denmark

Abstract

This paper urges that Laurence BonJour fails to make the case for an all-out a priori fallibilism "as clear as anything philosophical could be." Firstly, the paper introduces a number of distinctions of vital importance to the relevant debate. On the basis of those distinctions, it is argued that several interesting a priori infallibilist claims are not targeted by BonJour's central a priori fallibilist arguments. After this, the paper confronts BonJour's arguments on their own terms, attempts to fairly regiment them, and ensuingly brings out their weaknesses, thus regimented.

1. Introduction

Rationalists agree that some substantial claims about the world[1] may be justified a priori, i.e. independently of sensory experience. Still, rationalists may show moderation along one or more lines, whose interrelations are not altogether obvious. E.g. rationalists may insist that the phenomenon of a priori justification does not call for the stipulation of any entities, e.g. abstract particulars located in some platonic Third Realm, which are unacceptable to any member of their opponents the empiricists. Call this *ontological moderation*. Or they may insist that the obtainment of a priori justification need not bring into service any distinct faculty of the mind uncalled for in any instances of a posteriori justification. Call this *psychological moderation*. Finally, they may insist that a priori justification does not quite measure up to the epistemic powers bestowed on it by its traditional adherents. Especially they may insist that a priori justification does not always bring with it knowledge. Call this *epistemological moderation*.

Epistemologically moderate rationalism has currently risen to prominence through works such as Plantinga (1993), BonJour (1998),[2] Bealer (1999) and Peacocke (2000). After all, the position holds obvious attractions. Surely, propositions such as <nothing is green all over and red all over at the same time> seem to concern our world in a substantial sense and seem justifiable for each of us without recourse to perceptual experience, testimony, memory or anything else remotely a posteriori.[3] And this impression lingers even if such propositions cannot be construed as *analytic*. Yet in the present intellectual climate ontological—as well as psychological—immoderation are severely frowned upon.[4] And it appears difficult to see how a priori justification could retain its classical epistemic superpowers, if subjects have no special faculties of rational insight at their disposal, or, with or without such faculties, any access to a special realm of states of affairs for which our mental grasp is eminently fit.

Still, I shall argue, the truth of epistemologically moderate rationalism is not as evident as some contemporary rationalists might wish for. I should stress that my goal is not to defend rationalism as such, or to present a convincing positive argument for a priori infallibilism. Rather, I shall aim to undertake two projects. Firstly, I shall attempt a thorough regimentation of a priori infallibilist claims. The main point of this being the following: Some form of epistemologically moderate rationalism would be established by establishing the actual existence of false a priori justified belief with a non-analytical content (in so far as knowledge is factive). And, as we shall see below, this is indeed the route taken by prominent moderate rationalists like BonJour. However, given my regimentation, the actual existence of such beliefs is fully compatible with the truth of several interesting a priori infallibilist claims. At least BonJour would then seem either to owe us an argument against the types of a priori infallibilism not targeted by his argument, or owe us an account concerning how he can afford to be agnostic with regard to them. Secondly, the paper aims to undermine the force of BonJour's most prominent arguments aiming to establish beyond any reasonable doubt the actual existence of false a priori justified beliefs.

In order to achieve its aims, this paper begins by laying down an understanding of the central notions of *a priori justification* and *infallibility*. It should be noted from the outset that the type of infallibility discussed throughout this paper concerns *alethic* strength, i.e. the ability of a priori justification to guarantee truth. In contrast I shall not discuss the ability of a priori justification to provide indefeasible justification. Even if truth-guaranteeing and indefeasible types of justification have been equally termed "infallible" in influential parts of the recent literature,[5] my preference is to conceive of fallibilty in purely alethic terms. I consider this preference in line with received usage.[6]

If my argument succeeds, this much will have been established: At least some moderate rationalists should not rest as confidently in their epistemological modesty as is currently the case.

2. The definition of a priori justification.

A priori justification may be broadly and negatively defined as justification (in some sense) independent of sensory experience.[7] Call this *the traditional definition*. From it alone, as BonJour has correctly pointed out,[8] it is impossible to see why one should insist on the infallibility of a priori justification: Independency of experience says nothing of alethic strength. However, BonJour moves swiftly to the claim that "it is not at all easy to see what the rationale for the historical belief in infallibility has been" and personally confesses to see no rationale not involving "gross fallacy."[9]

The traditional definition is a descriptive definition: It points us towards the phenomenon of a priori justification by specifying something true of all its instances, namely independency of sensory experience. As such, in order to function properly, the definition must be at least extensionally adequate. And to serve philosophical purposes, it has better be intensionally adequate as well, in the sense that we can allow no possible counterexamples to it.[10] But, importantly, the traditional definition does not even begin to inform us, concerning any source of experience-independent justification, what makes it justificatory in the first place.

Thus, BonJour's cry of obvious fallacy is far from obviously justified. Surely there is no conceptual link from independency of sensory experience to infallibility. But infallibilist rationalists are hardly committed to stipulating such a link. Arguably, traditional rationalists such as Descartes did not put their great confidence in just any experience-independent source of justification. They put their trust in very specific source of justifications allegedly known from intimate experience, which, in the relevant sense, also happened to be experience-independent, hence a priori. Having thus hopefully opened my readers' eyes to the possibility that a priori infallibilism may not be swiftly dismissed as grossly fallacious, I shall continue to lay down an understanding of the notion of infallible justification useful to the present context.

3. Infallibility and a priori justification

In this context, let a source be any process leading to the formation or sustainment of a belief. No restrictions shall be put on such a source operating voluntarily or consciously. Readers may substitute "belief-forming/sustaining process" or "method" for "source" throughout, should they prefer. Nothing essential depends on terminological preferences here.

Two vital pieces of terminology, however, are these: Let an *infallible source* be a source that cannot result in belief without yielding a true belief (understand "employed" here as not requiring in any sense willful or intentional employment.). In contrast, let an *infallible belief* be a belief, which cannot be held, if false. Thus an infallible source may well yield beliefs which are not infallible. For a source to be infallible it is enough that beliefs be true, whenever flowing from that relevant source.[11] Remark, also, that infallible beliefs need not be necessarily true. It is enough that they could never be held when false.

I shall assume that any a priori justified belief is justified by virtue of its originating from some relevant source. At least I assume that any rationalist would agree to that assumption.[12] Call such a source: A source of justification (relative to the relevant justified belief). To exemplify: Descartes held clear and distinct [mental] perception to be an infallible source of justification. In so far as our firm convictions flow from that source, according to Descartes they are also justified and true. But notice that no rationalist need suppose that all infallible sources are also sources of justification.

In line with the traditional definition of a priori justification, let an a priori source be a source not involving any kind of sensory experience (memory of former sensory experiences obviously included). Historically, Descartes also took clear and distinct perception to be an a priori source of conviction.[13]

The above observations go to show two things: First, one would seriously underestimate the rationalist agenda, if one argues as if epistemologically immoderate rationalists would be content to establish the infallibility of *some* a priori source or other. It is the infallibility of *a priori sources of justification*, which is of key epistemological concern, i.e. whether some a priori sources *justifying* the beliefs flowing from those sources are also infallible. Secondly, BonJour does not quite hit the mark, when he canvasses the radical rationalist as going by "a genuine awareness ... of the necessity or apparent necessity of the proposition" after considering this proposition with "a reasonable degree of care."[14] As laid out above, infallible sources need not concern necessary or even apparently necessary truths. In fact it is not even obvious that they need concern infallible beliefs. It would take further argument to establish that, which, however, I shall not hope to provide here.[15]

With the above in place we may specify four versions of a priori infallibilism in order of decreasing strength:

1. Strong modal a priori infallibilism: Any possible source of a priori justification is infallible.
2. Strong a priori infallibilism: Any actual source of a priori justification (past, present future) is infallible
3. Weak a priori infallibilism: Some actual source of a priori justification (past, present, future) is infallible.
4. Weak modal a priori infallibilism: Some possible[16] source of a priori justification is infallible.

Here (1) $\Rightarrow$ (2) $\Rightarrow$ (3) $\Rightarrow$ (4), but not the other way around. One could easily complicate things a lot more, e.g. by indexing the notions of justificatory force and/or infallibility to the employment of some source by some particular epistemic agent under some particular circumstances. However, I see no point in introducing such complications in the present context.

It is debatable whether any actual rationalist has clearly committed herself or himself to (1). Still (2) is arguably implicit in e.g. Descartes' preferred source of believing by "clear and distinct perception of what I affirm" in his *Meditations*[17]: Not only does Descartes regard this source as infallible and a priori. He also sees no justificatory alternatives to it, at least in the actual world where he undertakes his meditations. But even if historical rationalists have focused on (2), the truth of (3) would still seem problematic to a rationalist with ambitions of general modesty. (4), on the other hand, is merely spelled out for reasons of completeness. It probably holds no independent attraction for rationalists.

The crux is that prominent contemporary rationalists such as BonJour have put much confidence in arguments for a priori fallibilism which, even if sound, would not establish anything beyond the falsity of (2). This is because such arguments are content to establish the actual existence of false a priori justified beliefs (with a suitably non-analytic content). Now, given the general commitments attributed to rationalists above, such a false a priori justified belief must owe its justification to a certain source (e.g. "believing by intellectual seeing/rational insight"). This means that at least one a priori source of justification is fallible, thus refuting (1) and (2). Still, (3) is left standing. And it would seem that moderate rationalists owe at least some account, either why (3) is false, or else why they are willing to remain agnostic with regard to those weaker a priori infallibilist claims.

It is beyond the present paper to discuss the metaphysical and psychological consequences of accepting (3). But it does seem a fair guess that it will prove hard for moderate rationalists to remain psychologically and metaphysically moderate to an uncontroversial degree, unless they are in a position to rule out (3).

This closes the first major part of the present paper. It has hopefully been established that even the world's best argument for the actual existence of false a priori justified beliefs (with a suitable non-analytic content) is insufficient to rule out all interesting a priori infallibilist claims.

Notice, however, that a priori fallibilists have not had much concern with weaker forms of a priori infallibilism, but have been content to target (2). I shall now aim to bring out that two of those arguments do in fact rest on rather controversial assumptions. I should stress, once again, that I do not thereby aim to offer any positive argument in favour of any type of a priori infallibilism. I only hope to bring out that, given the current market for a priori fallibilist arguments, the appropriate attitude towards strong a priori infallibilism does not seem to be the supremely confident dismissive stance adopted by Laurence BonJour.

4. BonJour's historical arguments

BonJour (1996) launches an argument which is apparently designed to carry in itself the full weight of his a priori fallibilist cause:

> It is as clear as anything philosophical could be that the claim of infallibility ... is false and completely indefensible. There are simply too many compelling examples of propositions and inference that were claimed to be objects of rational insight, and hence to be justified a priori, but that subsequently turned out to be false or mistaken. (1996, 111)

Arguably, in the above passage a brisk *reductio* of a priori infallibilism is intended. The passage does not offer much material, but the following regimentation seems fair:

1. If strong a priori infallibilism[18] is true, it would very rarely happen that a proposition was claimed to be an object of rational insight and later turned out to be false.
2. But it has often happened that a proposition was claimed to be an object of rational insight and later turned out to be false.
3. Hence strong a priori infallibilism is false: There are false a priori justified beliefs.

In order to charitably allow this argument maximal force against strong a priori infallibilism, let us interpret "rational insight" here as denoting any allegedly infallible a priori source of justification. Now, surely the second premise is more than plausible: The history of mathematics and philosophy is littered with salient examples of people claiming to rationally see some proposition to be true, only to be later refuted.

It is the first premise, which seems puzzling. From the infallibility of a certain a priori source of justification it does not obviously follow that believers are also infallible with regard to the question whether or not a certain belief does in fact flow from that infallible source. In the case of rational insight, BonJour does nothing to rule out that, in the cases where rational insight was claimed on behalf of a false proposition, the agent was in fact mistaken with regard to the question whether rational insight really occurred. Obviously, a long discussion could now follow regarding the plausibility of postulating such systematic mistakes. In the present paper, though, it will suffice to notice that BonJour does in fact gloss over a very contentious issue. Thus, his above argument hardly establishes the falsity of strong a priori infallibilism "as clearly as anything philosophical could be."[19]

Perhaps in recognition of defects like those brought out above, in 2002 BonJour offers the following passage, which clearly harbours a more elaborate argument:

> ...[I]t is hard to see how any human cognitive process could be entirely free from the possibility of error. (...) Moreover this general reason to suspect fallibility is strongly reinforced by what seems to be actual mistakes, including routine errors of calculation and reasoning, apparently clear, but paradox-inducing insight in logic and mathematics, and at least many of the errors that the history of philosophy is littered with. (...) A proponent of infallibility might perhaps insist that the apparent *a priori* insights from which the erroneous judgments resulted were not genuine, that genuine *a priori* insight is and must be infallible. But apart from any clear rationale for this claim, it is inherently futile if *a priori* insight is to be viewed as a basis for *internalist* justification in the way that the Cartesian view and most historical rationalists insist. If mock a priori insights at least sometimes cannot be distinguished from genuine ones by the person who has them, as the cases of error seem to plainly show, then the consequences of saying that justification results only from genuine insight will be that a person will be unable to tell whether or not a belief is justified on this basis – until its truth or falsity is established in some other way, making the justification supposedly provided by the insight no longer essential. (2002, 96–97)

This more elaborate argument is not as easily regimented as the 1996 argument[20]. I hope that the following regimentation will prove fair to BonJour's intentions. In effect, the argument is construed as a reductio; an attempt, based on premises with an internalist leaning, to force the strong a priori infallibilist into absurdity:

1. No source of justification justifies, unless the relevant believer is also justified that this source of justification was operative (a version of internalism concerning epistemic justification[21]).
2. If, in the case of a priori justification, justification that a source of justification was operative be not obtained by an a priori source, the relevant belief is no longer *essentially* justified a priori. [Definition of essential a priori justification.]
3. Hence, strong a priori infallibilism implies that, for any *essentially* a priori justified belief p, the agent's belief in p's justification is also justified by an infallible source (since, according to strong a priori infallibilism, any justificatory a priori source is infallible.) [From (1) & (2)]
4. People often believe that they justifiably believe some p by an a priori source (e.g. genuine rational insight), even though p is in fact false.
5. Even when granting to strong a priori infallibilism the infallibility of rational insight, *the best explanation* of (4) is the hypothesis that to the believer the presence of such rational insight is often indistinguishable from the mere appearance of such insight.
6. If, to the agent, the presence of such rational insight is often indistinguishable from the mere appearance of such insight, the agent cannot *infallibly* justify a priori that genuine rational insight were present.
7. Thus, to strong a priori infallibilists, beliefs justified by rational insight cannot be *essentially* a priori justified. [From (3) & (5) & (6)]
8. Hence, with regard to any proposition p, at least part of the justificatory work demanded by internalism in order for an agent to justify belief that p, cannot be done by an infallible a priori source. [Explication of (7)].
9. Hence, strong a priori infallibilists must either denounce the possibility of essential a priori justification, or admit that sometimes believers falsely, but a priori justifiedly believe that one of their beliefs flow from an infallible a priori source (such as rational insight). From (8)
10. But strong a priori infallibilists, by definition, cannot admit that any a priori justified belief is *fallibly* justified.
11. Hence, strong a priori infallibilism must denounce the possibility of essential a priori justification. [from (9) & (10)]. And this is absurd.

Notice first that there is no way to turn an argument of this type against weak a priori infallibilism (and, plausibly, BonJour has no such ambition). For surely a weak a priori infallibilist would allow that the second-order justification required by BonJour's internalism could be obtained by a *fallible* a priori source of justification. A weak a priori infallibilist could therefore take the more palatable horn of the dilemma set up in (9). But, it is time to move on to the discussion of the above argument and assess its merits in refuting strong a priori infallibilism.

The first problem concerns the premise (2) and BonJour's notion of *essential* a priori justification. In the passage quoted above, BonJour maintains that "the consequences of saying that justification results only from genuine insight will be that a person will be unable to tell whether or not a belief is justified on this basis – until its truth or falsity is established in some other way, making the justification supposedly provided by the insight no longer essential." But why should an adherent of strong a priori infallibilism commit herself to this? She need only insist that no a priori source plays a role in the justification of any belief unless that source is infallible. But this is perfectly consistent with the claim that any justification that that infallible source was used, cannot be obtained by an infallible source, hence, by the lights of a priori infallibilism, must be obtained a posteriori. BonJour of course seems to welcome this possibility. Still, *pace* BonJour, the infallible first-order a priori justification could, in a very natural sense, remain *essential:* There could be no way in which the believer could obtain justification for the relevant belief *entirely* on an a posteriori basis. In other words, it would be perfectly consistent for a strong a priori infallibilist internalist to maintain that certain beliefs may only be justified by some infallible a priori source, together with some *fallible* a posteriori source affirming that the relevant belief flowed from the relevant infallible a priori source. In such cases it seems hard to argue that the justificatory role played by the a priori source was somehow "inessential" to the justification of the target belief.

To sum up this objection: BonJour ultimately impales the strong a priori infallibilist on the unpalatable first horn of the dilemma set up in (9) in virtue of wedding her to his own stringent conception of essential a priori justification. But really, the strong a priori infallibilist-cum-internalist is free to see the justificatory importance of infallible a priori sources as resting in their co-operation with fallible a posteriori sources of meta-justification, when justifying beliefs by virtue of such a co-operation.

Another key problem concerns BonJour's implicit use of an inference to the best explanation in accounting for the truth of his plausible empirical premise (4) on behalf of the infallibilist. This step is brought out in premise (5) of the present regimentation. But here BonJour seems tacitly to rely on the symmetry of the indistinguishability relation: Really, all the strong infallibilist needs in order to explain the truth of (4) is the hypothesis that, often when agents experience *apparent* rational insight, they are unable to internally detect that they are not experiencing *genuine* rational insight. This hypothesis surely suffices to explain why, in such cases of apparent rational insight at least some agents are prone to believe that they experience genuine insights and testify to that effect. But in order to make his argument work, BonJour needs to saddle the strong a priori infallibilists with a very different commitment: He needs to commit her to the claim that the best explanation of (4) is the hypothesis that, when agents experience *genuine* rational insight, they are unable to tell a priori that they experience such genuine rational insight rather than an *apparent* rational insight. But BonJour fails so say anything underwriting, why the strong rationalist should adopt this very different hypothesis as her best explanation of (4). Instead we may presume that he simply holds uncontroversial the following symmetry principle: If mock insight can never be distinguished from genuine (allegedly infallible) insights, infallible insights can never be distinguished from mock insights. But this is far from clear. If e.g. some, but not all, genuine insights have a phenomenological property (say a certain lustre) possessed by no mock insight, and the subject invariably believes by insights with this lustre, it may well be that she can never tell, when confronted with a mock insight, whether this insight is genuine or mock, but will often believe by it nevertheless, also falsely believing that a genuine insight was present. But still she may, when confronted with a genuine insight with the right lustre, invariably believe by it. Provided that the genuine insights are factive, all it would take now in order to infallibly believe by the appearance of genuine insight would be to learn to form beliefs only when the appropriate lustre is present. And to satisfy internalism, also the subject could learn to believe that her belief is justified by way of rational insight, only when the appropriate lustre is present. The fact that people have often taken a mock insight to be a genuine insight (BonJour's plausible empirical premise) speaks nothing against the possibility or plausibility of the above.

Still, the above may seem incredible to some readers. An analogy might help. Suppose we consider a very different cognitive task from that of identifying true propositions by way of rational insight: The task of identifying beeches among the trees of a certain forest. And suppose, further, that we undertake this task in order to build a set of beech wood furniture for a discerning customer. We would lose the customer, if the order delivered contains even the slightest bit of elm wood. Our customer is very exacting about that. So we hope to search out the beeches *infallibly* in the following sense: Each tree of the forest, which we mark out as a beech, better be a beech. Now certainly, we would be frustrated if, each time when we confront a beech, we are unable to tell whether the tree is a beech or an elm. We cannot have that. At least sometimes when we confront a beech, we must be certain that it is a beech. However, we are able to live with our inability to tell, when we confront an elm, whether it is in fact a beech or an elm. We can also live with our inability to tell, concerning many beeches, whether they are elms or beeches. What we must do in order to achieve the desired type of infallibility is to mark as beeches only those trees of which we are absolutely certain they are beeches and leave the rest unmarked. We easily risk overlooking a lot of beeches in this way, but this is irrelevant. As long as, by the end of the day, all trees marked as beeches are in fact beeches, everyone is happy.

To speak in the language of this analogy, the a priori infallibilist may maintain against BonJours argument that we have indeed at our disposal a belief-forming mechanism that marks off certain truths, but no falsehoods, with a certain phenomenological lustre. And insist further that this mechanism acts as a source of justification for belief in the truths so marked. Other beliefs may *seem* a priori justified in virtue of *appearing* as if marked out by this lustre to the undiscerning "inner eye," but are in fact not justified at all. Finally, she may well attribute the fact that many have invested their confidence in false propositions based on the apparent presence of this lustre, to the fact that, even if one is not in doubt concerning its presence when the lustre actually appears, one may easily think it present when it is not: Even when we have at our disposal a source that will guarantee that all the trees we mark as beeches are in fact beeches, and even though we have no other reliable indicator of beech-hood at our disposal, if we are not very careful, we may still end up marking an elm as a beech.

So it would seem that there is no obvious way, based on BonJour's key empirical premise (4), to present a conclusive case against an internalist version of strong a priori infallibilism And of course, even if, arguably, traditional a priori infallibilist rationalists like Descartes were strongly committed to internalism, there seems to be no principled reason, why a strong a priori infallibilist could not prevent BonJour's argument from even getting off the ground by embracing externalism. All in all, based on BonJour's actual arguments, it would seem that the case against strong a priori infallibilism is still not as "clear as anything philosophical could be."

5. Conclusion

I hope to have shown that BonJour has outstanding work to do in conclusively defending his epistemologically moderate version of rationalism If my conclusions are correct, BonJour would need to substantively bolster his arguments before the case against strong a priori infallibilism is indeed "as clear as anything philosophical could be."

Some may generally object to this paper in the following way: At best you have pointed out a few problems for BonJour to fix. But no version of a priori infallibilism can be right. Firstly, BonJour and other moderate rationalists intuitively have the upper hand, when contending that "[I]t is hard to see how any human cognitive process could be entirely free from the possibility of error"[22] Secondly, epistemological immoderation threatens to bring along psychological and ontological immoderation. And these cannot be reconciled with our current scientific world image.

In reply to such objections, I must stress again that my purpose was not to defend rationalism as such. Neither was it my purpose to positively establish any kind of a priori infallibilism, let alone defend the strong version of a priori infallibilism arguably embraced by classical rationalists such as Descartes. Whether epistemological immoderation really commits one to psychological and/or ontological immoderation is not for me to probe here. Only I have stressed the need to keep those very different types of immoderation properly apart. And I hope to have established that, given rationalism, an all-out a priori fallibilism is not as well-supported by positive argument as is claimed by one of rationalism's most prominent contemporary adherents.

Notes

1 Of course there is room for disagreement concerning what it means for a claim to be "about the world." Some may want to restrict that notion very narrowly to claims entailing the existence of worldly particulars (property-bearers). Here, however, a wider sense is intended, in which e.g. a colour incompatibility claim such as "nothing is green and red all over at the same time" is about the world in so far as it taken to say something of the possible distribution of worldly properties.
2 Widely credited with introducing the term "moderate rationalism" in its now standard meaning of epistemologically moderate rationalism in the sense preferred here. See e.g. Aune (2002).
3 And such examples remain poignant even if, as argued by Beebe (2008), BonJour's more elaborate arguments in favour of the possibility a priori justification are viciously circular.
4 Benacarref (1973)'s famous worry concerning the ontological basis of mathematical knowledge is instructive in that regard.
5 In the vocabulary of Albert Casullo, the present paper consequently discusses only so-called "c-fallibility," i.e. the absence of guaranteed truth, Casullo (2003, 56). "P-fallibility," i.e. the defeasibility of justification, I shall not discuss here. However, as should be clear below, p-fallibility easily translates into my preferred idiom in the following way: A source of justification is p-infallible, if it delivers indefeasible justification.
6 According to the *Oxford English Dictionary* "fallible," when applied to "rules, opinions, arguments etc." means: liable to be erroneous, unreliable. On the other hand, nothing in the OED indicates the appropriateness of using "fallible" in the sense of indefeasible. Stable URL: http://dictionary.oed.com/cgi/entry/50081926?single=1&query_type=word&queryword=fallible&first=1&max_to_show=10 retrieved online 28 April 2010.
7 Russell (2007, 1).
8 BonJour (1998, 111).
9 BonJour (1998, 111).
10 Se Gupta (2008) for a canonical account of "intensional adequacy."
11 Although infallible beliefs are the most obvious candidates for the output of an infallible source, this is by no means conceptually necessitated. One need only presume here that true belief contents do not (in general, at least) have their semantic value *essentially*. E.g. the proposition <the tallest man in the world has brown eyes> is currently true, but could possibly have been false now and may well become actually false, when the man pres-

ently tallest dies. Thus, it is an open possibility that some infallible source produces beliefs which are not infallible, since they are false in some worlds, where the relevant source is impossible. A possible rejoinder: No infallible source could fail to produce beliefs with essentially true contents. Answer: Bad call. Whatever proposition it is that my though that I exist relates to, this proposition is hardly essentially true. But simply thinking it seems an infallible source of affirming the corresponding belief.

12 In a nutshell, this assumption follows from psychological explanations being causal explanations together with a respect for the basing relation warmly embraced by BonJour (2002, 245): "In order for a belief to be justifiedly held by a particular person for a given reason, the person's recognition of that reason must be part of the psychological explanation of why the belief is held." In the terminology preferred here, no belief is then justified unless flowing from a source broadly specifiable as recognition of a sufficient reason.

13 Some further observations of interest, but without immediate concern to the point of the present section: It is a small step to the claim that not all infallible a priori sources need be sources of justification. E.g. there could be a source in no way dependent upon sensory experience, which yielded only infallible beliefs. But obviously, it would be a contentious claim to argue that those beliefs were justified simply due to flowing from such a source. Remark, that rationalists are no way committed to such a claim. Also, even if trivially all necessarily true beliefs are infallible, not all infallible beliefs need be necessary. Traditionally certain beliefs whose content refers to either the believer or the belief itself have been taken to be contingent and infallible. The Cartesian "I am a thinking [incl. believing] thing" may serve as a case in point. David Kaplan's so-called "theorems in the logic of demonstratives" such as "I am here, now" provide alternative examples Kaplan (1979).

14 BonJour (1998, 114). See also Bealer (1996, 6) for a very similar focus on "seeming necessity."

15 For some infallible source M employed by epistemic agent A and some [true] belief B of A produced by M there could easily be a possible world w, such that B is false in w and A did not believe B by M in w. Of course this could be ruled out by restricting belief contents to propositions with rigid truth conditions, i.e. beliefs having their actual semantic value in any possible world. This restriction, however, seems entirely arbitrary.

16 The kind of possibility here could be specified further, if one is not a modal monist: naturalistic possibility, metaphysical possibility etc. As (4) is too weak to attract any rationalist, however, such qualifications is a mere academic exercise.

17 Surely Descartes would have balked at the claim that anything beside "clear and distinct perception of what I affirm" (Med. III, 35) could have yielded any degree of sense-independent justification whatsoever.
18 For a definition, see above.
19 I thus recommend at least mild doubt about (1), flying against BonJour's strong conviction in its truth. Obviously, it would have been better, had I pointed to strong reasons to reject it. But this is beyond the project of the present paper.
20 An autobiographical note: Before settling on the present regimentation, I toyed with several very different readings.
21 If only in the weak sense that any call for second-order justification is internalist. However, in another sense such a call may obviously be warranted on externalist grounds: E.g. one may hold that epistemic justification amounts to production by a reliable mechanism and also argue that no belief is thus produced without meta-justification being also produced.
22 BonJour (2002, 96).

References

Aune, Bruce (2002). "Against Moderate Rationalism." *Journal of Philosophical Research* XXVII: 1–26.

Bealer, George (1996). "On the Possibility of Philosophical Knowledge." *Noûs* 30, Supplement: Philosophical Perspectives: Metaphysics: 1–34.

Bealer, George (1999). "A Theory of the A Priori." *Noûs* 33, Supplement: Philosophical Perspectives, 13, Epistemology: 29–55.

Beebe, James R. (2008). "BonJour's Arguments against Skepticism about the A Priori." *Phil. Stud.* 137: 243–67.

Benacerraf, Paul (1973). "Mathematical Truth." *Journal of Philosophy* 70: 661–79.

BonJour, Laurence (1998). *In Defense of Pure Reason: A Rationalist Account of A Priori Justification*. Cambridge: Cambridge University Press.

BonJour, Laurence (2002). *Epistemology: Classic Problems and Contemporary Responses*. Lanham: Rowman & Littlefield.

Casullo, Albert (2003). *A Priori Justification*. Oxford: Oxford University Press.

Gupta, Anil (2008). "Definitions." *Stanford Encyclopedia of Philosophy*, stable url: http://plato.stanford.edu/entries/definitons/

Kaplan, David (1979). "On the logic of demonstratives." *Journal of Philosophical Logic* 8: 81–98.

Peacocke, Christopher (2000). "Explaining the A Priori: The Programme of Moderate Rationalism." In Paul Boghossian and Christopher Peacocke (eds.), *New Essays on the A Priori*. Oxford: Oxford University Press, pp. 255–85.

Russell, Bruce (2007). "A Priori Justification and Knowledge." Stanford Encyclopedia of Philosophy, stable url: http://plato.stanford.edu/entries/apriori/

Sellars, Wilfrid (1963). *Science, Perception and Reality*. London: Routledge & Kegan Paul.